DAVID BOWIE

SERIOUS MOONLIGHT

DAVID BOWIE'S SERIOUS MOONLIGHT

☾

THE WORLD TOUR

☾

PHOTOGRAPHS BY DENIS O'REGAN

TEXT BY CHET FLIPPO

DESIGNED BY J.C. SUARÈS

GRAPHICS BY MICK HAGGERTY

☾

A DOLPHIN BOOK
DOUBLEDAY & COMPANY, INC.
GARDEN CITY, NEW YORK
1984

Copyright © 1984 by Stenton, S.A.
All Rights Reserved
Printed in the United States of America
First Edition

Photos on pages 90-91 © Don Hammerman
Production: Caroline Ginesi
            Laurence Vetu
            Kathleen Gates
Coordinator: Roy Finamore

Set in Bauer Bodoni, Bodoni Book and Ultra Bodoni
by Leland & Penn, Inc., New York

LIBRARY OF CONGRESS CATALOGING IN PUBLICATION DATA
Flippo, Chet, 1943-
   David Bowie, Serious moonlight.
   1. Bowie, David. 2. Rock musicians—England—
Biography. I. O'Regan, Denis. II. Title.
ML420.B754F57 1984 784.5'4'00924 [B]
ISBN 0-385-19265-7
ISBN 0-385-19266-5 (pbk.)
83-40140

SERIOUS MOONLIGHT

hen Doubleday, the publishers of this book, asked for my own feelings on the Serious Moonlight Tour '83, my mind panicked. My thoughts shuttled back and forth through a plethora of emotions: American ecstasy and depressions. European familiarity and isolation. Eastern promise and suspicion. How on earth could I compress such an abundance of images and impressions onto a few pages? The old diary trick! That should do it. Let instant thoughts and sensations summarize it all. Describe one day and hope that would provide a partial idea of touring in 1983.

SINGAPORE

Whenever the faces of stewardesses blanch gray-white with fear, and the overhead cupboards open and spill their contents, I hold my little metal Buddah tight and press the crucifix to my chest and tell myself it's just another airplane landing. As near-hurricane winds knock about the inevitable D.C. 10 and pea-soup clouds annihilate even a fantasy of visibility, I hold back the urge to scream, and I remember how bad driving in New York can be these days. But then, even before I have formulated these thoughts into pure terror, the clouds are sucked upward and away, and we are two and a half inches above the waters of Singapore.

For me the Eastern leg of a tour is always the carrot. For the rest, however magical the chemistry of the performance, the day-to-day mechanics of getting from city to city are draining and monumentally boring. That's the stick.

During the cab ride to the Ming Court Hotel, I direct a string of unrelenting tourist questions at the driver. Where's the old part of town? Is this the Arab or Chinese or Malay section? Why are they pulling down all the picturesque stuff? He lets me know in no uncertain terms that the new apartment blocks with their bathrooms and air conditioning are

A FITTING FOR MADAME TUSSAUD'S WAX MUSEUM IN LONDON

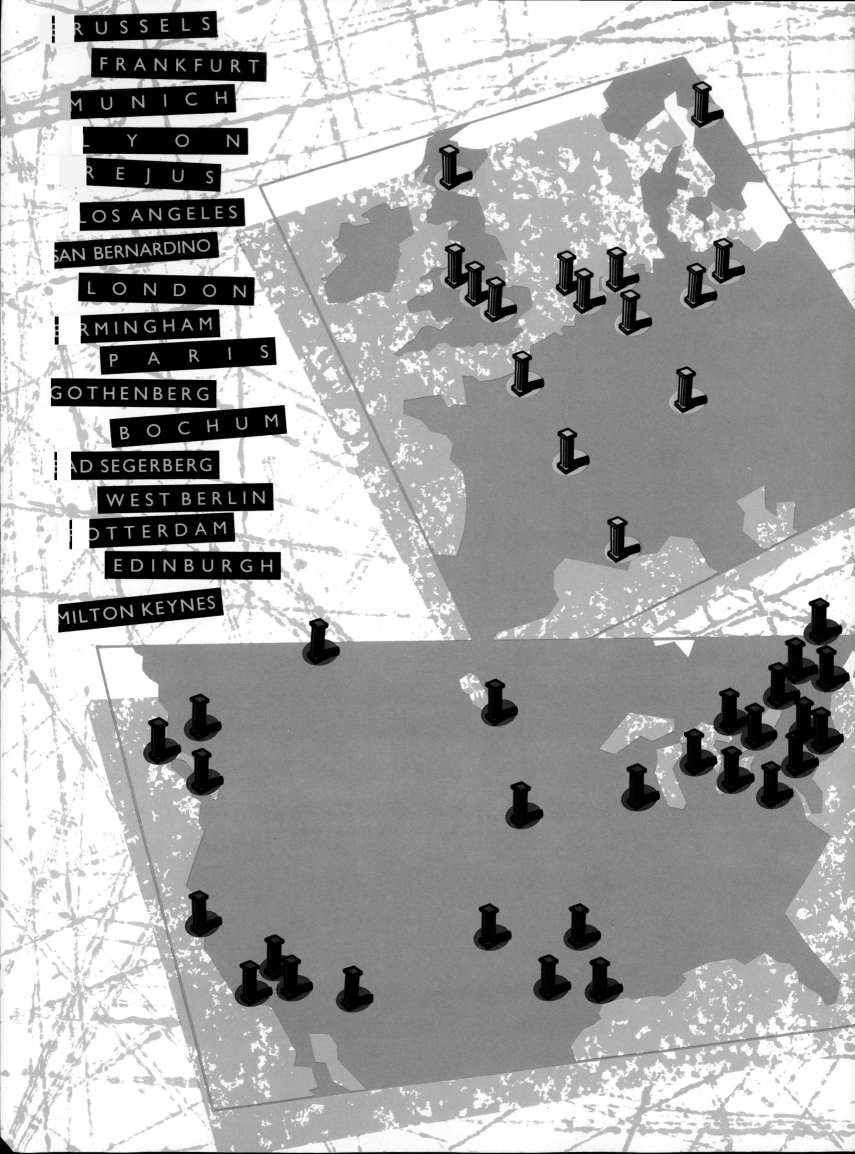

BRUSSELS
FRANKFURT
MUNICH
LYON
FREJUS
LOS ANGELES
SAN BERNARDINO
LONDON
BIRMINGHAM
PARIS
GOTHENBERG
BOCHUM
BAD SEGERBERG
WEST BERLIN
ROTTERDAM
EDINBURGH
MILTON KEYNES

QUEBEC CITY
MONTREAL
HARTFORD
PHILADELPHIA
NEW YORK CITY
CLEVELAND
DETROIT
CHICAGO
EDMONTON
VANCOUVER
TACOMA
PHOENIX
DALLAS
AUSTIN
HOUSTON

NORFO
WASHINGTON D.C.
HERSHEY
BOSTO
TORON
BUFFA
SYRACU
ANAHEI
VANCOUVE
WINNIP
OAKLAN
TOKYO
YOKOHAMA
OSAKA
NAGOYA

PER
ADELA
MELBOURNE
BRISBA
SYDNE
WELLINGTON
AUCKLAND
SINGAPO
BANGKO
HONG KONG

far more in favor with families of five or six than are the rat- and cockroach-infested unsanitary slums that I take as local color. I'm crushed. He then goes on to tell me about the recent drug-related hangings. "Many people hang one day. Fourteen years old up to seventy. Death just for smoking the hashish. We clean up town."

The driver also lets slip how hard it is for him to keep up with the relentless upward spiraling cost of living. He hasn't ever had a holiday and thinks he may have taken a few days off work about four years ago. "But everybody work," he says. "Singapore will be next Hong Kong."

When I move into my suite at the Ming Court Hotel, the little Malay porter indicates the three-tone carpet, the ten-channel T.V. He is bursting with pride about the bathrooms but is visually awed by the three hundred square feet of personal freedom. He paces the room from wall to wall. "So much space," he sighs.

The Singapore authorities are not friendly toward rock & roll. Two of my songs, "China Girl" and "Modern Love," were banned from radio play. "Restricted," as they say. Our wonderful and fearless promoter, Dr. Goh Pohseng, risked his livelihood, bank balance, and even his freedom to get me and my band into his country. When the authorities heard I was going to do an impromptu guest appearance at his youth club two days before our major gig, they busted it, banned the resident band for indecent performance, and threatened Dr. Pohseng with imprisonment if a guest of the club—(me)—should get up on stage and sing. He also faced incredible local resistance in getting the staging and lights together. When he asked for three yards of cable, local suppliers—knowing it was for rock & roll—would only sell him a 100-yard drum. No one would lease him timber for the stage, so he ended up buying an architect-designed permanent structure at ten times the cost . . . and so it went, over and over.

The lights were flown in from all over Malaysia. Many arrived broken, and those intact not much more powerful than a bedroom lamp. But, good lord, he tried.

I am supposed to say something to the children in the Singapore audience. These children who are doomed to ride the up escalator forever. These American-designed fiber glass light-conducting interested-inscrutable faces. I stand on a beautifully improvised high-tech kitchen-unit stage, and I am shocked at how loose-eyed and shoddy my songs seem in the face of the fact that these green- and red-streaked kids represent a thousand-year-old culture. As if in agreement with the cultural differences, the local authorities have separated me from the kids with a 65-foot ramp between the first row and stage. I do mean kids and I do mean separated!

I rip through a welcome and an introduction to the band in Chinese. It is received with dutiful sympathy by the crowd as my pronunciation is so dreadful that not one word is understood. The audience end of the ramp is so far away from the band that I am singing half a beat behind them. I look back and see a tiny, jumping Carlos Alomar leading a badly lit rock & roll group. I peer out and see paramilitary cops at the ratio of about one to two with the first row. They finger their billy clubs, their hands on their guns. My jacket style is designer Tokyo—skyscrapers and diamante searchlights. There is so much lacquer in my hair that a hurricane couldn't move it. My shirt is held into my pants by elastic thongs round my legs. I have two pairs of socks on because of oversized shoes. I am imploring the crowd, "put on your red shoes"...there is a scream of recognition—15,000 strong. A tiger-print-clad girl is slapped back over the security boundary by a ferocious swing of a billy club.

In a city where you can be arrested for chewing gum, a demand to put on red shoes is deemed unhealthy.

The warm night air bathes our bodies, and the scents and smells of the East grow stronger as the evening grows longer. For a moment I feel I am playing to the tiger-infested jungle that existed here until the arrival of concrete a few short decades ago. There is an audible breakdown of reserve as curious uplifting faces recognize this song, then that one. They are singing along. It is an overwhelming experience for me and for any artist, I suppose, to see an audience of a culture ostensibly so far removed from one's own, singing along. It may not should like a big deal, but for one night it can mean everything.

Now we are all dancing and loving each other and having the greatest of times. We are back for an encore, and the crowds swell up over the ramp. We touch hands and inspire each other on. All at once my songs sound very good, and I get another elusive glimpse of how lucky I am to be doing what I do. I think I may tour again.

So now I pass from my notebook to the writing of Chet Flippo and the camera work of Denis O'Regan as they give you their own impressions of a rock & roll tour of the world in 1983.

CHAPTER ONE

Present at the Creation

ER GROSSEN NACHFRAGE

PEN AIR
erious Moonlight
DAVID
BOWIE
CONCERT '83
24. Ju

Freitag, 24. Juni 1983
Offenbach
Fußballstadion
Einl.: 18.30 Uhr, Beg.: 20.30 Uhr

Karten an allen bekannten Vorverkaufsstellen erhältlic
Tickets available at USO Frankfurt and Wiesbaden or your local re

TELEX

```
⊕
.2162983 rmda d

to: mr. wayne forte
c/o ramada renaissance hotel
serious moonlight tour

approval for db  visa is in  shoud be in
contact ms. spencer at us consulate  app
nyc-n-88148.  please call her and let her
by to pick up.
regards,
kg
itg  649378
us counsalte number is 499-9000
⊕
2162983 rmda d
1639 Q6/16
via trt
```

ELCOME TO THE WORLD of FutureRock. You there! Welcome! You in the carefully bleached, authentic Levi's 501s and the starched-to-a-crisp-just-bought-T-shirt-bearing-the-face-of-an-Idol and the honest-to-God (and hideously expensive) three-striped Adidas scuffs intended to be running shoes. But—isn't it true—the only time that you run in them is frenzied moments like this one, when the house lights in Brussels' Forest National Hall are dimming. Dimming, along with your chances of finding a choice seat near the stage before the magic hits. So you run, Adidas scuffs barely touching the floor as they glide across outstretched feet of the 8,000 fortunate fans provident enough to buy advance tickets for this May 18, 1983, show, maybe suspecting that this was a significant event: *"le retour du grand blond,"* some said as they rushed from Paris to Brussels. One was actually heard saying, *"Funky et chic"* as he settled into a prime seat and reached for his sterling silver flask to offer sips of calvados to fellow chic-funkers.

But all you know, cher-fleet-of-Adidas-foot, is that you came to Brussels attracted by you know not what, exactly. You have no idea that this is a Major Event, and you are clearly not interested in listening to theories about same. You just want to get the hell close to the stage. And then reach into your Levi's watch pocket for your carefully-rolled-just-for-this-show little stick of grass and fire it up and jump up and down as you wait for it to turn your brain into a devil spiral when the music washes over you. All you know—*"Je m'excuse"* you mutter as your Adidas-wings trip over outthrust shiny white boots—is that something reached out and grabbed you by the scruff of your neck and shook you unmercifully and told you to get the hell to this show. That's why you stammer as you answer why you had, *had* to be at this show: "Because."

Because? That's what they said about Elvis and Buddy Holly and the Beatles and the Rolling Stones. Because? Well, that's generally been a good enough reason for fans (as in fanatics) to follow the True Rock & Roll Way. You, Levied wisp of a child stumbling through crowded aisles toward a Holy Ark of a stage, are—and you don't want to know it—another step in the evolution of rock & roll. A convert to FutureRock who perceives Elvis—if at all—as analgous to the

God and man no confessions
God and man no religion
God and man don't believe in modern love

MODERN LOVE

US FESTIVAL MADNESS: ARE YOU RIGHT WITH GOD, BROTHER?

DAVID AND BILL ZYSBLAT ON JET 24

Spanish-American War and Snooky Lanson. But, rock & roll forges ahead, just as you do in your unstoppable rush to stage front as houselights fade and lights of an unearthly glow flow slowly across that stage. You weave to and fro when you get to your square foot of precious space and as wave after wave of sound washes over you and, judging by the new spark that imbues your eyes, if there is indeed such a thing as the Spirit of Rock & Roll, it has just taken over your entire being and soul.

"La Bowietude." Yep. That's what this new rock is being called. La Bowietude. The reason being—as you, Mr. FutureRock, slip into your BowieWorld and gently leave us behind—the reason being that as of May 18, 1983, in the Forest National Hall in Brussels, David Bowie came roaring back with a vengeance to reestablish his rock & roll turf and to redefine what rock & roll might be about as it stutters into the Eighties and dreads the Nineties and ignores The Big 2000. Welcome, wisp of an Adidas child, to FutureRock.

La Bowietude. Indeed. I can't think of a better way to describe the interlocking, misty rings of influence and mystique and following and fans and fallout that trail behind this David Bowie. If I didn't know better, I might think that La Bowietude meant a way of life, or at least a certain approach to life. And I think I might actually be right, judging from a cross section of the Bowiefans I encountered. But you, gentle-Bowiefan-in-Adidas-scuffs-entering-a-trance-during-"Heroes," did you know that the humble 8,000-seat beginning of a tour that no one really expected would do what it later did? Of course not. No one did. I didn't, you didn't, promoters didn't, David Bowie maybe didn't, other groups and singers certainly didn't (especially when they had to reroute their tours to avoid going head to head with a Bowie date in any city). What I mean to delicately say, gentle-gate-crasher-but-devout-Bowiefan, is that this tour was hot shit. As in Hot Shit. Nobody but the Stones could come close to Bowie before. This time, he left them in the shade. Perhaps that's why he christened this the "Serious Moonlight Tour" (but then again, perhaps not). But, as your left Adidas is not so gently removed from your left foot by the rough boot of the Alsatian gate-crasher lurching against you during "Let's Dance" and your general euphoria prevents you from noticing that you are now only half-shod, you should know that "Serious Moonlight"—hell, you don't have to know anything. You're having a good time, which is the only real demand any truly serious person ever asked of rock & roll. But you might be interested to learn that Serious Moonlight attracted so many truly serious people that it became humongous. Let's trot out some figures to impress the half-shod.

Serious Moonlight first trod the boards in Brussels on May 18 and ran through 96 shows in 59 cities in Europe, North America, and Asia before winding down in Hong Kong on December 8, 1983. That's 12,270 minutes of music—in 2,208 songs—played for 2,601,196 members of the Truly Serious in 15 countries. Mainly for future generations (and for Trivial Pursuit followers), why not reel off some more numbers? The largest show was for 80,000 in Auckland, New Zealand. The big festival crowd was 300,000+ at the US Festival. The smallest show was before 2,120 of the ultra Truly Serious at Hammersmith Odeon in London. Tour members flew 3,787,000 miles with only 7,788 pounds of luggage (spread among 177 bags). The longest flight was 23½ hours from Nice to Los Angeles; the shortest, a 15-minute hop from Buffalo to Syracuse, N.Y. Serious Moonlight employed—however briefly—12,245 people, and they drank 35,720 cans of soda and beer. They filled up 9,457 hotel rooms. Tour equipment weighed 64,000 pounds. All the tickets for the tour weighed 5,224 pounds. And—but enough. Backward reels the big mind until it crunches to a stop: so what does all this mean? Why are socialites in major cities jousting for Bowie tickets? Why are people I have not heard from in 20 years suddenly calling me and begging for Bowie tickets? Why is Bowie on the cover of *Time?*

Why not?

What else is happening around the world in rock or even pop music? Michael Jackson has yet to become this year's Pet Rock. Boy George is still but a gentle swish in the wings of the much-vaunted and eventually ineffectual second British Invasion (of bands, that is). The first Invasion involved the likes of the Beatles and the Stones. And, of course, Gerry and the Pacemakers and the Searchers. And on and on. David Bowie, born David Jones, was failing to make a huge impact on American audiences with such records as 1964's "Lisa Jane," by Davie Jones with the King Bees. In 1965, he was David Jones as lead vocal of the Manish Boys—the name being a cop of a Muddy Waters song—and Davy Jones (and the Lower Third.) He was a bit of a fop, but it was obvious that he knew what he was about. His *Space Oddity* caused a bit of a flap: obviously inspired by the movie *2001: A Space Odyssey,* Bowie's central character, Major Tom, is the ultimate astronaut who defects and chooses terminal alienation once he has a taste of outer space. Bowie continued to be a critic's darling and simultaneously a bit of a puzzle to the U.S. record-buying public. After the first story on him appeared in *Rolling Stone,* people actually used to ask me about "the guy who looks like Lauren Bacall." Enough of that for now.

So not much was happening, rock-wise and pop-wise when 1982 turned into 1983. No one in the rock mainstream really expected a Bowie boom. K-Tel, the TV marketing giant, had issued sixteen Bowie cuts as *The Best of Bowie,* in December of 1980; this was not at all a bad record, but it was a piece of history. And nothing in rock & roll is more poison than being labeled "history." That's like trying to tell a 14-year-old about World War II or Elvis or even the Beatles. Past tense and very tense. David was not a commercially happening guy. His last RCA album, *Scary Monsters* (1981), sounded great but sold like three-day-old scrod. Many rock insiders totally wrote him off. He put together a group of songs that would become the *Let's Dance* album and called up the

PHOTOGRAPHER DENIS O'REGAN AND
GLENIS IN DALLAS

great producer Nile Rodgers to produce it and, recklessly but confidently, decided he would, by God, do a world tour. Whether or not the world was ready for it.

He was ready, by God. That's all that it took. That's the true spirit of rock & roll.

Tell David that tonight. He's happy as he paces the plush-carpeted aisles of his chartered Boeing 707 Starship that's slicing through a black velvet sky somewhere way above North America. Roiling clouds are thousands of feet below the thin, pale jet that's distinguished only by slim red and blue stripes that seem to race around the fuselage and by bold black letters that spell out JET on the tail. Life on the plane is a bubble that seems unbreakable and invincible, a floating model of the way things should be. Captain Woody is young and hip and walrus-mustachioed and a crack jet pilot; the flight attendants are hopelessly hip and beautiful/handsome; the food is amazingly fresh cracked crab and surprisingly authentic tamales and groaning trays of fresh fruit and drinks galore. In the forward and rear cabins, those weary travelers who are not gorging themselves on chocolate mousse are watching movies on video players. Life could be worse.

One of the passengers reclining in the forward lounge is a slender, blond man who looks younger than his 36 years. His face is a study in camera-ready planes and angles; his eyes—one blue and one gray (Hey, he's got "Civil War-type Eyes")—establishing a commanding presence. He is now dressed in mufti: comfortable khaki shirt and olive trousers. A couple of hours earlier, he had been dressed to the nines in a dandy's dream of a Forties silk suit, and he had broken the house record of 11,285 paying customers in Quebec City's Colisée de Quebec (he pulled in about 14,400). That was the first date of his first North American tour in five years, a certain return to the uncertain world of rock & roll.

But he lounged comfortably on the streaking Starship, reclining on a couch and reading aloud to members of his band from *The Book of Failures*. He laughed about such failures as the jury that sat through an entire trial before admitting that they were all completely deaf. "Read this," David laughed, "you'll like it. Heard of the Not Terribly Good club of Great Britain?" Sax player Steve Elson, lolling across the aisle, said to Bowie, "You should do a book of rock & roll failures." "That's too long a book," I said. Bowie laughed and said he would have to start with The Legendary Stardust Cowboy. Since I know the Legendary, I started singing "I met my true love down in the wrecking yard," and Bowie chimed in with me. Then David took a solo and leaned forward—at 30,000 feet—and sang the only Superstar version that I'm sure I'll ever hear of the Legendary's "Gemini Space Ship." This is now Bowie singing: "I took a trip on a gemini space ship, and I thought about you-oo."

"That guy was incredible," David said. I was amazed that he had even heard of the Legendary, since he never sold more than about ten records, but then David laid out a blockbuster: "I took the name Ziggy

Facing Page:
REHEARSING AT LAS COLINAS, OUTSIDE DALLAS, TEXAS

Following Pages:
DAVID BEING GREETED BY FANS AFTER REHEARSALS IN JAPAN

Stardust from the Legendary Stardust Cowboy," he said. The internationally chic Ziggy Stardust character and persona sprang from an eccentric whose only venue was a drive-in burger joint in Lubbock, Texas. The Legendary Stardust Cowboy was universally ignored as he stood on the hood of his car and howled. He really did. He recorded two 45 singles for Mercury Records, and the Mercury person who recorded him was called on the carpet pretty damn quick. But the Legendary was the first cosmic rocker. Welcome, as it were, to show business. How perfect that David Bowie sought him out. No fool, he.

Is this truly David Bowie, the first rock & roll boulevardier, the man of a thousand masks, a mystery wrapped in an enigma surrounded by a riddle? It seems to be so. This is David Bowie, born David Jones in 1947 in Brixton, become rock & roller extraordinaire. He's worn many mantles: Ziggy Stardust (the before-his-time extra-terrestrial), the prophetically chic Thin White Duke, the exquisitely chic Diamond Dog, and on and on. Now he seems to be just plain David Bowie, bringing an amalgam of his music that could define the rock & roll of the Eighties. He offers, if you will, a warm and accessible show that throws rock-hard American rhythm & blues up against the Euro-techno-pop that Bowie pioneered, along with his flair for visuals that predated video rock. What's happened? A dozen years ago, he was considered so weird that his Carnegie Hall debut could only be achieved by endless negotiations and much pressing of the flesh. Now? David Bowie is the standard against which others are measured. Who changed? How did straight-ahead rock & roll come to be praised by critics as a total performance art experience as opposed to a minor nuisance back in the Sixties? Good questions, all.

And not many answers forthcoming, but I don't blame Bowie for not waltzing out every morning with a press conference. One British press clip I have in front of me screams: "Bowie! An Intimate Story of Drugs, Riches, Sex...And Genius." If you really want to know how the scurrilous press goes about its business, consider this opening paragraph: "Half man, half alien. A drug addict. A singing skeleton. The pop world's outrageous, crazy chameleon." That was the standard Bowie view. Now? Perhaps there's nothing like an ideal whose time has come. The world was ready for David Bowie, and fortunately, David Bowie was ready for the world.

Well, Mr. RockFuture, as you finally wander out of Forest National, euphoria intact, Bowie T-shirt limp with sweat (never did find your other Adidas, did you?), you're pretty self-satisfied with your Idol, aren't you? Hell of a show, right? Spectacular lighting and sound, topnotch musicianship and great performance by Bowie. All's well again in the fragile world of rock & roll. But did you ever wonder just how a world-class concert and tour like this happens? Of course not. The only time you ever think about anything that happens offstage is when you try to sneak backstage and Callahan or Big Tony nabs you and suddenly reverses your field of motion. You just kind of think, vaguely,

Facing Page:
"ASHES TO ASHES" PERFORMED IN BRUSSELS

The return of the thin white duke
throwing darts in lover's eyes
Here are we one magical moment
Such is the stuff from where dreams are woven
Bending sound

STATION TO STATION

BIG TONY CHECKING OUT HAMBURG

that Bowie and these musician guys just kind of show up at a hall and put on a show. Then they go back to the hotel and dive headfirst into a pit of finest cocaine dotted with an even dozen nude, nubile young bimbos, right? And that's the essence of rock & roll, right? I wish it were so, and so does every rock musician I ever met. Unfortunately, there's a hell of a lot of hard work and sweat and nose-to-the-grindstone involved. And you might like to know about it. So forget the sex and the drugs (for now) and pay attention for a while. You might actually learn something.

David Bowie decides to tour after a five-year hiatus. So what happens next? He just has to show up at the hall and do a quick show, right? No. There's a little more to do than that. From his manor in Scotland, where he lives a quiet existence, David started planning a major world tour. It's not unlike a strategic military mission. You need musicians, instruments, costumes, a stage, choreography, a lighting system, a sound system, trucks and roadies to handle tons of equipment, bookings in the best venues you can find in some kind of logical geographical progression (you do *not* want to play Paris one day and Cleveland the next and London the next), hotel rooms somewhere comfortably near the venues, cars and vans to move people and materiel around, either the crazy-quilt system of commercial airline bookings for a couple of hundred people or else a chartered plane and careful ground transportation, passports and visas for everyone, landing permits in different countries, some kind of banking system to handle pursing and disbursing large amounts of money from one country to another, a security system, counterfeit-proof tickets for each city, counterfeit-proof backstage passes for each show, lists of VIPs and lesser mortals to be invited to each show, lists of press and radio and TV representatives, and on and on and on, down to details so mundane that you don't want to read about them because they have nothing to do with the (supposed) glamor and glitter of high-powered rock & roll on the road. How many cold cuts and *crudités* and bottles of Perrier and Heineken and Tab and Evian Water should be ready backstage? What if David breaks a shoelace in Syracuse? Where can you find an English-speaking doctor at 4 a.m. in Berlin? Is there a 24-hour dry-cleaners in Gothenburg, Sweden? How many extra guitar strings are enough when you're playing Fréjus? How will you do the mounds of laundry? Is there a 24-hour dentist on call in Lyons? Can you get 16 rolls of gaffer's tape and a dozen AC fuses and three Stilson wrenches and a left-handed Phillips screwdriver in Rotterdam at 5 a.m.? Have the police departments in every city been contacted, so that a Bowie invasion will not take them by surprise? Mundane questions, surely, unless it's your tour that hinges on them.

So what you do, if you're David Bowie, is decide what you want done and assemble a task force to run things for you. Bowie is his own manager and basically delegates tour functions on a contract basis to the best people available. Isolar sent out feelers: Bowie will tour; are you interested in working the tour?

DAVID'S DRESSING ROOM IN FRANKFURT

CARLOS ALOMAR, THE BANDLEADER

The foundation of the tour was provided by what might be called the "57 Street Troika" in New York City. West 57 Street in Manhattan contains, per square foot, more show business people than any other spot on earth. For the Serious Moonlight Tour '83, Bowie homed in on 57: Bruce Dunbar his business representative and Gail Davis, director of creative services at 57th and Broadway, Wayne Forte at 57th and Seventh Avenue became booking agents and tour coordinators and Bill Zysblat at 57th and the Avenue of the Americas was tapped to be tour director.

Bill Zysblat is an affable accountant who runs a successful company called Sound Advice on the fourth floor of the Directors Guild Building, next door to the New York Deli. You might not peg him for a rock & roller—a rather pale and impish accountant— but his office walls are lined with gold and platinum albums from such grateful clients as the Rolling Stones and David Bowie. One busy day, he sits behind his cluttered desk and noshes at a corned beef on rye for lunch and ignores the angry winking lights on his telephone and talks about the Bowie tour. "Basically, the day after Bruce told Wayne and me that we were retained to do the tour, we sat down and carved up a pie of things to do. Wayne is a booking agent, and my company is a business management firm. He did bookings, and we handled the money. Then we had 40 to 50 other areas where we had to find the people with the most expertise. Charter plane, hotels, and so on. We put out the word that we wanted competitive bids. I had Brent Silver, who used to work for the FAA, and his machine fly around to about 12 different locations and literally take apart the engines of all the charter planes bid on, and they interviewed the pilots and reviewed the records of the companies and literally found us the safest airplane.

"Same thing with travel agents. Same thing with auditioning band members. The most time-consuming thing was the legal structuring of the tour. David is a British national performing around the world and being produced by a New Jersey corporation. I've got a flow chart that covers 300 or 400 agreements for the tour. It's an amazing piece of work. The man-hours put into the business end of this tour—just to get David and his equipment in and out of different countries—is just incredible. Like, our plane can fly from London to Paris but not from Paris to Lyons, because that would be taking business away from a local carrier. Sometimes the airport permits would get cleared two hours before we took off. And we're just sitting there sweating.

"The other pretour problem is cash flow. We have to pay up front for everything. Hotels, airports, everybody wants their money up front. Everybody's got a deal to negotiate, there's always another deal to cut. Right down to how to print the backstage passes. Should they be reflective so they can't be Xeroxed? I decided finally to put a slight flaw in the backstage passes that only the security people would be alerted to. The same thing is true of all the tickets to all the shows. They have tiny flaws that only we can discern. But a ticket-taker can tell *immediately* when he tears the ticket whether it's a fake. There are literally billions of little details like this." Bill wearily pushes aside his

Preceding Pages:
THIS IS "SPACE ODDITY" IN FRANKFURT'S FESTHALLE

CARLOS AND DAVID IN "WHAT IN THE WORLD" IN MUNICH

GRACE JONES TURNED UP BACKSTAGE IN
PARIS

C
―――
42

BACKSTAGE IN LA. GAIL DAVIS INTRO-
DUCES DAVID TO GINA SHOCK AND KATHY
VALENTINE FROM THE GO-GO'S, WITH
HOWARD HESSEMAN LOOKING ON

uneaten sandwich and finally addresses himself to the angry blinking lights on his phone.

It's a short stroll down 57 to Wayne Forte's International Talent Group offices, which are even more frenetic than Zysblat's. Phones ringing off the walls, a palpable tension in the air. A front office—overlooking 57 Street and, on the hazy horizon, a green slice of Central Park—has been designated the David Bowie Production Office. On a stifling day, when it's 95 degrees outside and the humidity approaches saturation point, the production office is helter-skelter with hustle and bustle. The little Airtemp air conditioner lodged in one window is wheezing away manfully, but it can't defeat New York's heat. The PO Coordinator, a striking blonde named Jamie Mosedale, is barefoot and glowing with perspiration as she treads the gray carpet between her phones and the Telex and the computer that links the office directly to the tour, via satellite. "We never close," she winks as she fields yet another call demanding choice DB seats. A few feet away, assistant coordinator Rica Fujihara talks on the phone in Japanese to Japanese promoters and then in French to French promoters and then in English to ask: "You're calling for tickets for Robert Redford?" She rolls her flashing black eyes as if to say "Heard this one before." She demands a call-back number—and woe be to any would-be scam artist who tries to hustle Mosedale and Fujihara. "We caught five ticket scalpers already," says Rica between calls, "and one of them claimed he was Wayne Forte."

Who is himself just down the hall, glued to a telephone and a computer. Wayne is what you would call an intense man, which is an understatement for any rock & roll booking agent. Urgent phone messages had formed such a huge pile that they had toppled over on his desk. Demo tapes were stacked everywhere. Gold records from ELO and Art Garfunkel gleamed on the walls. Wayne, with his taut features and sculptured beard, finally turned off his phones—reluctantly—for a few minutes, to talk about the tour.

"What happened," he said, "was that, when Bill and I got involved, I sent off Telexes to all the European promoters, all the guys that David had worked with in the past and that I had plus some new people who had heard about the tour and were excited. I arranged meetings for January [1983] and Bill and Bruce and Gail and I met from 10 a.m. to 10 p.m. every day for six days at the Carlton Towers in London with promoters. It wasn't like a meat market; we just wanted to find promoters who were as excited about this tour as I was. Then they'd go back and sell their markets. And would sell the tickets. There were some promoters who would come in and go, 'Yeah, OK, I'll do this tour, but I'm also doing Supertramp and Rod Stewart.' I said, NO: you don't understand! This is gonna be the biggest tour of '83. This is *David Bowie!* He hasn't toured in five years." In his Manhattan office, Wayne's voice carried the emotion that he obviously had conveyed to the European promoters. The Bowie apparatus, while still feeling out Euro dates, decided to schedule a press conference for David in London

THE PARIS SHOW BROKE MANY ATTENDANCE RECORDS

DAVID AND BRUCE DUNBAR IN A BANQUET
IN JAPAN

☾

44

to announce the tour. So dates had to be inked in. The tour grew.

"Originally," Wayne said, "my tactic was to set up the first three weeks of the tour, with all the major indoor dates. It was a hard sell in Europe, especially outdoor dates. Promoters felt David wasn't an outdoor act and was a reserved-seat act for an older, well-dressed audience, that kind of thing. Our concept, as we discussed with David, was to do the indoors to set up the outdoors. After we announced the major indoors at the press conference, we got 250,000 ticket requests for 44,000 seats. So we knew we could go outdoors. Kids in Gothenburg, Sweden, were camping out for days for tickets. We ended up doing 58,000 or 60,000 a day there. And then things went crazy. The promoters went wild. They wanted the biggest stadiums. In his whole career, David had only played outdoors once, and that was in Australia, five years ago. So this was a whole new thing."

The tour, which was a modest projection at first, grew like an avalanche, building and building on itself. "We started with a piece of clay, and it got molded into a big ball," Wayne said. "Whatever it was going to be anyway, I will never know. It might not have been this big. Projecting it down the road; that's the trick."

And if you're wrong? "You can't afford to be wrong," Wayne said seriously.

Just a stretch down 57 Street, up in the gray-carpeted walls of Isolar, Bruce Dunbar said pretty much the same thing. Gold and platinum Bowie albums crowded each other on the walls of his hushed office. Bruce is a serious man, wearing Serious Preppy: boat shoes, gray flannel slacks, *serious* striped blue shirt with a fashionably thin, suitably electric blue tie. He's earnest and sober as he says, "I approached it all from the financial end. I think that was my forte, in terms of being able to say to David...um, he thinks of things from the pure, the artistic end. I've contributed to him in the respect that I've freed him up to pursue his artistic goals. Historically, what happens in most cases is that an artist has a manager who then hires a production company or whatever to take over the tour. And the manager takes on that role. In my case, I'm not a manager. David manages himself. That's one of the aspects that is unique to David, in that he really does make his own management decisions."

That he does. Once he made up his mind to tour again, he did so with a single-minded vengeance. Imperial commands (requests, actually) went to the best people around who can put a major rock & roll tour on wheels and make it work. He himself started seriously working out with a boxing instructor to get into fighting shape for the tour.

Artist/designer Mark Ravitz was toiling in his Brooklyn studio when he got his royal summons. Ravitz had gotten caught up in the whole rock coil back in the Sixties when he was a student at a branch of the New School on Second Avenue in Manhattan's Lower East Side (then euphemistically dubbed "The East Village"). Directly across the grubby expanse of Second Avenue was New York's rock cathedral: the Fillmore East. Art students and rock & roll have always been an

DAVID WITH BRIAN GYSIN IN PARIS

"Voici le Bowie 83 pour tout Paris"

Rebel Rebel you've torn your dress
Rebel Rebel your face is a mess
Rebel Rebel how could they know
Hot Tramp I love you so

REBEL REBEL

inevitable mix. Ravitz got caught up in the heady flow and went on to do pioneer work in rock staging. His "Diamond Dogs" set for Bowie was a classic flux of rock's urgent and simplistic one-dimensionality and of the careful, studied, paced all-dimensioned world of architecture, design, and theater. So it was no great surprise to Ravitz when he was asked to fly to Bowie's on a day's notice to meet with Bowie. They discussed Bowie's model for a Serious Moonlight stage design. Ravitz flew back to Brooklyn and in a few days was ready with a more elaborate scale model of a stage set. The finished version of the plans went off to the seasoned rock-thing-building-and-trouble-shooting-company FM Productions of San Francisco. FM, among doing many other things built the stage for the 1976 Democratic Convention in Madison Square Garden and attracted much admiration for the innovative bomb traps it built into the stage. Bomb traps? Yes. If a bomb was heaved onto the stage, there were slanted inclines where it could be quickly kicked or shoved into a trap door and thence dropped to a fairly bombproof chamber below stage. Some other secrets must still be kept. This much-sought-after company was also retained to handle the too-hot-to-handle 1984 Summer Olympics in LA. You know they took good care of Bowie.

So, the stage was secure, the plane was secure, the bookings were

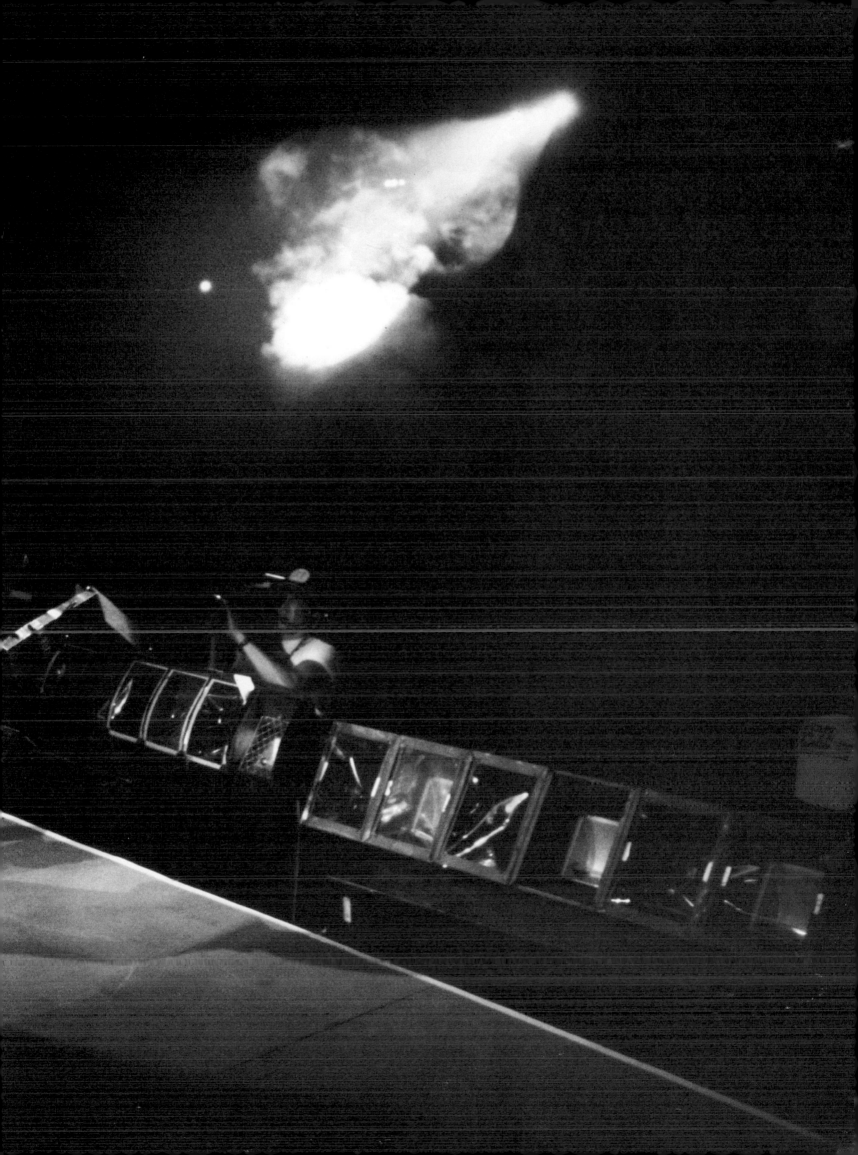

secure as far as bookings can be; things were gradually falling into place. Sound and lights and trucks and food and hotels and such were being attended to by a carefully picked personal staff. Old Bowie hand Carlos Alomar (who wrote the song "Fame" with Bowie and John Lennon) and Bowie set about putting a touring band together. Bowie, who had pioneered the technosynthesizer-puréed sound adopted by so many second-generation European techno-pop bands, decided he wanted a full, basic rock guitar-guitar-bass-drums bedrock augmented with a keyboard fill, a three-man saxophone wall, and two backup vocalists. "First," said Carlos, "he decides on the people he uses. Then he leaves it up to me and I decide. On this one, he had a lot of musicians he'd already used on the album. He didn't have to try them out; he knew they could cut it. The ones he didn't have, I filled up."

The group: guitarist and musical director Carlos Alomar, credits including John Lennon and Bette Midler; drums, Tony Thompson, from Chic, Blondie, and Diana Ross; lead guitar, Stevie Ray Vaughan, much heralded blues virtuoso from Texas and just signed by John Hammond Sr., no less, of CBS for a solo album; bass, Carmine Rojas, from Stevie Wonder and LaBelle; keyboards, Dave LeBolt, from Billy Joel and Steve Hackett; saxophone and wood synthesizer, Lenny Pickett, stalwart of Tower of Power, Rod Stewart, Little Feat; sax and woodwinds and synthesizer, Steve Elson, from Boz Scaggs and Johnny Otis; sax and woodwinds, Stan Harrison, from Diana Ross and Southside Johnny; vocals, Frank and George Simms, two albums on their own, plus backing for Chic and Peter Frampton. A fairly solid crew, it seems. A broad-based coalition that would bow to no one in being able to deliver Bowie's current elegant funky rock dance music.

Carlos is as close to Bowie as any musician will ever likely be. They first met when Carlos was asked to play for Lulu sessions being produced by David Bowie. Lulu he had heard of; David Bowie he had not. When Bowie hired him, Carlos was with the Main Ingredient. And he invited Bowie, then a glow-in-the-dark-red-haired-oddity, up to the Apollo Theater to see the Main Ingredient. Bowie charmed everyone.

Bowie and Carlos trust each other. Carlos is a natural musical leader because of his easygoing but firm temperament and his impeccable musicianship and sense of timing. He also, as Bowie obviously recognizes, bridges the increasingly different worlds of black and white pop music as well or better than anyone around.

"So," Carlos said about this tour, "after the band was selected, David and I got together and decided what songs he was gonna do. He presented me with 35 songs. And then we go into rehearsal. We learn 35 songs in two weeks. And then we get together with the lighting and sound and with David." Rehearsals started at a small studio in Manhattan and then moved to a full-blown dress rehearsal in the wind-swept plains between Dallas and Fort Worth, Texas. Out in the flats there is a hesitant city-of-the-future known as Las Colinas, huddled around artificial canals and an artificial lake. There's also an

Preceding Pages:
PERFORMING BEFORE ABOUT 500,000 AT THE US FESTIVAL

LONDON'S HAMMERSMITH ODEON, BY NIGHT

Facing Page:
PARIS BY SUNSET MAKES A LONG TOUR WORTHWHILE

"LET'S DANCE" GOT ALL PARIS IN A FEVER

Preceding Pages:
THE CROWD IN PARIS, PERHAPS THE TOUR'S
MOST INTENSE

Facing Page:
RED SHOES WERE SOLD OUT IN EUROPE
BEFORE THE TOUR BEGAN

enormous communications complex the size of Hollywood, something originally intended to replace Hollywood. Great sound stages and all that. The complex is perfect—all major rock bands have discovered —for rehearsing with ultimate technical facilities and zero public distraction. And a four-star hotel within gondola distance (speedboat distance, in Texas). Bowie and company worked hard for weeks. No distractions. The closest restaurant outside the hotel was a canalside vaguely Victorian structure that housed a McDonald's. The enticing skyline of Dallas, though it glowed as brightly and flirted as saucily as it could, was too far away for a quick pleasure dip. That meant that there was a lot of time for a lot of work: musicians learned charts and even choreography; lighting sequences were planned; lighting people lighted and looked; sound people listened. The auxiliary forces knew exactly what they had to do—which was rehearse.

And rehearse. And once more.

First just the rhythm section, so drums and bass and rhythm guitar can hope to hear each other once they're in a stomping, pounding arena. Then keyboards and lead guitar, who can't hear each other across the stage even in rehearsal, let alone in concert. The horn players and vocalists figure out where they fit in. And the computerized lighting has to be programmed fairly closely to a perfect micro-second or else it's going to look pretty damn foolish. And the sound has to be there. This is, after all, top-of-the-line rock...& roll.

"It's just day-to-day analysis," Carlos said. "Sometimes things happen so fast onstage that I have to go back and listen to the tapes and hear the whole arrangement. See who's screwing up and where. All I can hear on stage is Tony [drums] and Carmine [bass], some of the horns, a little bit of keyboards. I have to look at David all the time. When I'm doing a show, I'm wide awake, looking at David's lips all the time, reading his lips, because I can't hear him at all. And I have to look back and forth at the other guys, to make sure they're not having any problems. Cause if, say, the drummer drops a beat they go out on a B chord and he drops a B—and it might be because he just broke a drumstick or broke a snare or his footpedal broke and his roadie's fighting to get it back before the next beat.

"So I'm thinking of that, and I'm thinking about giving the band its cues and giving David cues and getting cues from David. And then playing guitar, dancing, and singing at the same time. There are so many things to think about onstage that I don't even know what I'm thinking about onstage. Just looking at David, and keying on him, that's about it. Sometimes, his cue is a blink. He drops one hand as a cue. The cues I give back are with the neck of my guitar: I pull it up, I pull it back, or down. Tempo back, tempo down. Everybody is grooving off the rhythm section. The synthesizer is sweetening things on top, and the lead guitarist is filling in, and the horns are just doing their blasts. But they watch me. If I pull my guitar neck to the left, that means: cut it off before time. If I pull the neck down, that means: *cut it off.* If David blows a second verse and jumps to a third verse, we have to *react.*

DAVID PLAYS GUITAR ON "YOUNG
AMERICANS" AT BAD SEGERBERG

Facing Page:
"YOUNG AMERICANS" AS DONE IN PARIS

"At a show, I have to check the sound and the lighting beforehand. I check out the kids, the crowd, to see what condition they're in: if they're in rain or if they're being crushed or if it's too hot or anything like that. I see how the police are, see if there's any harassment. I check whether a local curfew may be a problem. I check the staging. If the show is outdoors, I check the wind factor and all that, air quality, how the sound carries. If there's too much dust in the air, David can't sing a long set, because it would kill his voice. So we'll change the set to include songs in a lower range or songs that will let him rest his voice

"Once we're on stage, all we can see is maybe the first two rows of the audience. That's the shame about the outdoor gigs: whoever is strong enough pushes up to the front. And after we play the first few notes, we can see the first three rows drop, as 100,000 people behind them start pushing. Then the next batch comes in, the 100,000 give a little push again. And they drop. And we're saying to ourselves, 'Oh, shit . . .' I remember at one show in France, they were coming through *under the stage.* They were waddling through, just like they came from *The Night of the Living Dead* with their eyes rolled back in their heads and they didn't know where the fuck they were. The front rows were getting hosed down. They finally picked up on one idea and picked up all the people who had fainted and passed them overhead to the stage. Scary, you know. And there were the slam dancers in Germany, these punk kids with spiked buckles and bracelets and knuckles and when they went to dance, they just slammed into people, spikes and all, and, man, they made a big hole in that sea of people out in front of the stage. That was a crazy five years ago. Now I think the audiences will be a little bit more grateful, or graceful.

"David took a real big risk in taking a five-year break in touring. That's a risk in any business, anywhere. So you hope for the best. David got off of that other record label [RCA] and he had an immediate obligation to EMI when he signed with them. The minute he signed that contract, on comes the road, on comes the touring David Bowie. But he changed everything else: the band, his office, everything. And he gets a best-selling record right away with 'Let's Dance.' And he gets a new young audience, 16-year-olds, who *love* that record. They might know *Scarey Monsters,* but they don't know who Aladdin Sane is or who Ziggy Stardust is. They just don't know. But I think they've heard of him anytime they hear anything about top-of-the-line rock. He's never seen but he's always mentioned. I think that's been his whole karma. And he's holding on to it. I know older people who say, 'I know I can depend on this man to deliver a good record; not like when I buy an album with only two good cuts.' And they know better than to miss a Bowie concert.

"And David is trying to meet these two forces. The older crowd and the younger crowd. On this tour, he's got to introduce them to his *music,* not to the man. This tour is like: 'David Bowie does David Bowie.' He's singing about the guy who wrote about these people. David

doesn't have to be anybody now, and he just wants to sing the songs that made him famous. Something for the mind's ear."

From Dallas, after the Las Colinas trials, the troupe winged off to New York to prepare for the European invasion. FM Productions shipped off the massive stage to Europe. Showco of Dallas dispatched tons of wiring and sound equipment. Showlites did the same with its lighting equipment. Advance teams of sharp technicians who would have been called hippies ten years ago descended on Brussels to wire up that city for a Bowie blow-out. Lawyers had visas ready. Hotels and caterers and ticket agencies (and ticket scalpers) and T-shirt franchisees and bootleggers (of records and tapes, that is) and car and truck rental agencies and various lowlife scam artists who pop out of the ground for every major rock tour and of course your everyday, ordinary ticket-buying-rock-fan public and all manner of rock phenomena were gearing themselves up all across Europe for this tour.

While JET was roaring up out at JFK Airport and the Bowie group was assembling on the sidewalk in front of a Manhattan hotel before heading for the airport, a slight shift occurred in the, well, what you might call the musical lineup for the tour. Texas blues whiz Stevie Ray Vaughan had played brilliantly on the *Let's Dance* album. No one contested that. But at the rehearsals in Las Colinas, there was a slight tension in the air that suggested that he was not entirely suited to be ...to be a team player behind a superstar for a world tour that might run six to eight months—especially after his attractive CBS Records deal.

It is certain that guitar whiz Earl Slick got an urgent call at his home in Davis, California, from a Bowie aide who strongly suggested that it would be nice if he could leave soonest for Brussels and start a world tour as David Bowie's lead guitar. Slick, who really is a top-line lead player and had worked with Bowie before, was on the next plane. *Fait accompli.*

"That was kinda like a time bomb," Carlos said cautiously about the situation. "I had been covering the parts that Slicky would do. And he [Vaughan] was just playing solo. In that case, I would have used another guitar. And this tour is like induction into the—it's like a six-month boot camp."

"BOWIE SELLING OUT EVERYWHERE."

Said *Variety:* "David Bowie's 1983 world tour—the singer's first in five years—has posted sellouts at every stop since it began in Brussels, Belgium, May 18...Indeed, if any single element has served to make the Bowie tour a unique entertainment event, it would be the under-fulfillment of the potential demand for performances by the willowy rocker."

This, ahem, willowy rocker proceeded to set Europe on its ear. His coming was anticipated, oddly enough, by women's shoe wholesalers. They *knew,* even before rock promoters did, that David Bowie was going

COFFEE BEFORE TAKING THE STAGE AT GOTHENBERG, SWEDEN

to be a hot property. Why? Because in "Let's Dance" Bowie advises women to put on their red shoes. And in his widely seen video of the same song, red shoes are a co-star. As a result, there·was a run on women's red shoes in Europe. Shoe stores were left rifled and exhausted. Such is the power of rock in the marketplace.

Before the tour, Bowie made a quick trip to Cannes for the film festival, where he was fêted for his role in Nagisa Oshima's film *Merry Christmas, Mr. Lawrence.*

Bowie was virtually held prisoner by the paparazzi. The rock mag photographers, who thought they owned Bowie, were trampled on by the world syndicate photographers, who felt Bowie belonged to the world. I suspect you can venture a guess as to the winners. The real winner, actually, was Bowie, since he is the first male rock superstar to be perceived, seriously, by the world film community as an out-and-out, no-nonsense Real Actor.

Brussels on May 18 as a tour opener was almost flawless. Bowie did a dress rehearsal the day before for tour photos. This was the first time The Tour Getaway was practiced, you know, the instant exit by Bowie and band after the show. Two days in Brussels and then off to Frankfurt and Munich for a few days. There were a few frightening moments when the crowds in Munich crunched the barriers in front of the stage. Later, there was also a very discreet skinny-dipping party at the hotel, while Bowie was off at a club called the Sugar Shack. A lot of people stood around and stared at him. The next day, it was off to Lyons, where it was cold and damp and dreary. Mildew on the walls, that sort of thing. The show, at the Palais Des Sports, was well received, even though Bowie's voice was hampered by a cold.

Bowie was staying in Cannes again, and left for a half-hour drive to Fréjus, where the venue is an old Roman amphitheater named Les Arnes. Actually, it's quite aristocratic, even majestic, when you regard it as a rock hall. When a glowing sunset softly gilds its noble, ancient pillars and the massive boulders that possessively protect the stage, it is nothing but the most beautiful rock hall in the world. Backstage, in the gentle air, Bowie works himself up for the show with a workout on his Everlast speed bag, which was suspended from a Showco equipment case turned on end. By the soft nightfall, there is a genuine festive, impish, and medieval atmosphere amidst the celebrants out front. Pan himself seemed to urge on the euphoria of a starlit rock & roll paean to joy.

The Serious Moonlight troupe was infected with that sort of stardust and spent the rest of the night fêting road manager Arnold Dunn for having achieved yet another (unnumbered) birthday, the celebration of which set back every single member of the tour at least a day. And those hangovers were jarred by the scene at Les Arnes on the second day. A whole lot of people from England and a whole lot of people from Italy and Germany and who-knows-where heard about the good times at Les Arnes and decided to try to join in. Including many people whose thrills are extra-musical. It was fairly tense until the guards with their

☽
63

Facing Page:
"CRACKED ACTOR" IN GOTHENBERG, SWEDEN

Following Pages:
DOING IT OUTDOORS AT BAD SEGEBERG, WEST GERMANY

Alsatian dogs lowered the excitement level a bit and screened out the obvious undesirables at the gates. Monty Python's, Eric Idle, Bowie's friend, and the members of Duran Duran came to the show, and Bowie met them for a drink after the show.

The next day is a neat rock & roll nightmare. Get up early. May 28, 1983. Get on a bus. Roll out through the mist. Stumble onto JET on the Nice runway. Takeoff, finally. Settle back and go to sleep in deep, plush, leather seats. Then be roughly shaken awake as you suddenly land in Brussels to refuel.

"Why do we have to refuel in Brussels?" "Nice has a short runway, and the 707 couldn't take on enough petrol to get you to Los Angeles." "What?"

Off to FutureRock, U.S.A. Off to the US Festival II or whatever it's called. Whatever, it called Bowie and Bowie answered and the answer was yes. He said he would play his first United States outdoor show ever. Remember how the Bowie 707 Starship had to take off from the short runway in Nice, after everybody was bused in to Nice at the last minute from Cannes? The flight crew got lost, you'll recall, so the plane was, oh, an hour and a half late taking off. Then, ha ha! it was short of fuel so it had to derail, as it were, in Brussels to tank up. It sucked in fuel to the tune of $45,000. And the gas man at Brussels demanded $45,000—*in cash*—from this helter-skelter-looking-bunch-of-gypsies-or-worse before he would clear the plane for takeoff. Zysblat offered his Exxon credit card to the authorities. They came back 45 minutes later and said that was insufficient. Zysblat finally bloomed and came into his own when he advised the officials that either they would take his personal check for $45,000 or he and the plane and Bowie and the tour were going to take off and sky away to Los Angeles and good luck to the police and all the Mirages and F-15s who tried to catch them.

"Did it work?" you ask.

Of course it did. That's why rock & roll exists. That is exactly what rock & roll has always been about. It works. And those who don't understand it fear and loathe it so much that it works doubly against them because of that fear and loathing. Unfortunately, the triumphant Starship was grounded for another two hours by bad weather.

By the time the Starship cleared French air space, it was maybe six-and-a-half hours behind schedule. Off nonstop to LA. Because of equipment problems, a new soundboard had to be hauled along for the US show. The only place it would fit on the plane was in the aft restroom, which was thus put out of commission for the duration. Which meant that the Starship's 40 inhabitants were limited to only the forward restroom. After 22 hours and counting, that restroom gave up the ghost. When Starship landed in Los Angeles, customs and immigration officials boarded, took one whiff, and reeled offboard. Now, the Starship was supposed to land and clear customs at LAX and then make the brief jump to Palm Springs, where the troupe would stay for the US thing which is out in the desert anyway. Here it is 9 p.m. at LAX, and customs has dumped *everything* on the plane (well,

BACKSTAGE IN BAD SEGEBERG, WEST GERMANY

everything but the toilets) out on the runway for inspection. The Palm Springs airport closes at 10: no way to make it.

The Bowie troupe of 40 people slumps morosely on the tarmac. The local health department arrives and boards the Starship, noses around and officially seals the plane shut. As a health hazard. The most glamorous rock & roll tour ever is forbidden to reboard its plane and is stranded on the asphalt after 22 or so hours of traveling, and huddles down like proud arrivees at Ellis Island. *This* is the Big Kahunga of rock & roll who jetted in here straight from Europe to headline before a crowd of at least 300,000? Yes? Yes! There is no more humbling experience than clearing customs, but if you are a certified international rock superstar, you can count on being more humbled than anyone else. As in, "Please assume the position."

"Pardon me?"

"The position, dammit. Up against the wall, you, uh, person." Your legs spread while you lean against the wall and not-so-gentle-hands shake you down for weapons or dope or worse. Meanwhile (as the tour experienced in Montreal) the drug-dogs sniff all the luggage, which had been spread across the runway. And the customs officials defiantly ask Bowie for autographs—"for friends." It's hard to imagine anything more glamorous.

Anyway, here at a remote corner of LAX, Bill Z. again rises to the occasion and finds a phone booth and quickly rounds up a limo to take David and Coco and Big Tony off to Palm Springs and then manages to charter a bus to haul everyone else. So the bus driver didn't know how to get to Palm Springs; Amy Grey was happy to back-seat-drive. After maybe 28 hours of nonstop travel, band and staff get to sleep. And maybe a few hours by the pool before heading off to the US 83 Festival, a cultural oddity set down in a literal dustbowl called Glen Helen Regional Park in a wasteland named Devore, California. Somewhere near Los Angeles, it goes without saying. US was a personal whim of Steve Wozniak, a founder of Apple Computers, a whim which cost him many millions of dollars. Supposedly, science fiction writer Ray Bradbury told "The Woz" he *had* to book Bowie. US's press release on Bowie was this: "DAVID BOWIE, whose genius, depth, style and originality have defied the music industry's obsession to place its non-conformists in verbal strait-jackets, will headline the third day. . . . It will be his first musical performance in America in half a decade." It was also his first musical performance to register in the seven-figure range, money-wise. Big bucks. It also cut the Euro-tour in half and presaged the tour of the States, but it seemed that the Bowie hunger was insatiable. He knew how to fill up and use the two huge DiamondVision screens that let most of the crowd actually see him as something other than a distant dot on a dusty horizon. He also finally realized the end, perhaps totality of Ziggy when he blazed and flamed through "Rock and Roll Star." No more a "wild mutation," Bowie now controls the situation. In any event, the US Festival was a Bowie watershed, the first time he had found the control to handle a few hundred thousand people. This is

☾

73

Preceeding Pages:
ULLEVI STADIUM, GOTHENBERG, SWEDEN

Facing Page:
THE CORRECT HAT TO WEAR IN BAD
SEGEBERG, WEST GERMANY

good training for a superstar. Everything else is pressclips after that.

Almost. There's still a nonstop flight back to pick up the Euro-tour after the US success. Bowie's set ended at 1 a.m., May 31. It took two hours for the Bowie bus to crawl through traffic to rejoin JET. Band and staff were pleased to find that Bowie had ordered an elaborate sushi bar for them. Then a 5 a.m. takeoff for London, where a sold-out three-night-run at Wembley Arena awaits. You finally collapse into bed at the Carlton Tower Hotel in Cadogan Place in London. Construction noise shakes you out of bed, until tour advance-person Eva Strom slips £50 worth of bills to the construction foreman. Instant silence.

Wembley was a Real Event, despite the lowering storm clouds that were grayer than the building itself. This was David's real homecoming to London, after five years gone. Apart from the "real" audience, celebrities lined six-deep up for the privilege of being there: Pete Townshend, Koo Stark, Sabrina Guiness, Keith Richards, John McEnroe, Terence Stamp, Jeff Beck, Carrie Fisher, Vitas Gerulaitis, Tom Stoppard, Paul Theroux, Rod Stewart. You get the idea. When David kicked the big world balloon out into the crowd at the start of "Young Americans," he said laconically, "Take better care of it." Earnest Bowieologists everywhere are still pondering the levels of meaning that statement carries. Writing on the Wembley shows in *The Observer,* Anthony Denselow accurately noticed that the "atmosphere of the crowded tiers was more often akin to Lourdes than to the usual rock-concert jostle in shabby Wembley."

Memo from tour publicist Alan Edwards to tour members:
"We have a mixed bag with regards to English music press reviews with good revew in *NME* and *Sounds* and a bad one in *Melody Maker* (smallest circulation out of the three by far as it happens)."

Off to Birmingham for two shows in two days. Then a quick flight to Paris, crisp, clean sheets at the Warwick Hotel, and two amazing shows that drew 120,000 people to the lawns of Auteuil. They came early and stayed late, despite the crackling atmosphere of a threatening storm. Jee Ling, who is the exquisite "China Girl," showed up for the first concert.

Off to Sweden. Gothenberg. Where one newspaper had already run an illustration of the floor plan of the Bowie floor of the Park Avenue Hotel. By the time the Bowie troupe arrived it was knee-deep in young women, and it stayed that way. Bowie had to sneak in and out through the hotel kitchen to shake the mob.

"All of Gothenberg was David Bowie's last night," ran the story in *Sydsvenska Dagbladet,* "when the rock star gave his first concert at Ullevi [stadium] in front of the 59,000 fans. The Rolling Stones' old record was beaten with a broad margin."

Aftonbladet said: "David Bowie turned Ullevi into a boiling pot of life, feast, and music. The event of the year in Sweden lived up to all expectations."

EYEBALL FITTING FOR MADAME TUSSAUD'S
WAX MUSEUM

And so it went throughout Europe. Biggest rock crowd ever in
Scotland, with 47,444 in Edinburgh. On June 30, Bowie performed a
surprise benefit concert at London's Hammersmith Odeon, proceeds
going to his childhood turf: the Brixton Neighbourhood Community
Association. He had last played Hammersmith ten years before and
had, in fact, announced his retirement then. Back again, and looking
good. The band did the show in their street clothes, Bowie sporting
white, Navy-style-brass-button-front-trousers, royal blue shirt, and red
suspenders adorned with gold anchors. He expanded his usual mime by
using an inflated (perhaps) human leg as guitar and saxophone.
Princess Michael of Kent had gotten a standing ovation at the
beginning of the show but, as usual, Bowie's was deafening at the end.
Paul and Linda McCartney sent a telegram: "Our daughters Heather
and Mary went to the Hammersmith Odeon show and if they are to be
believed, you are pretty hot stuff. Thanks for thrilling them."

Euro-tour wound up with three frantic nights at Milton Keynes, a
mammoth bowl in a new-town setting outside London. It was hot and it
was sweaty but 174,984 paid £10 and £11 to push in over three nights.
The band especially liked the gig because of the Space Invaders video
games backstage. Bowie had fun onstage, at one point stopping to hold
up a set of keys he said had been tossed onstage. "I've got a front-door
key to a mansion in Belgravia, a safe-key, and a key to the girlfriend's
apartment. Whoever threw them, please raise your hand." Everyone of
course did. "You wouldn't want them," Bowie laughed. At show's end, a
crane hoisted the tour's huge inflatable half-moon-shaped-blimp-
balloon above the crowd. As its eyes winked on and off in brilliant blue,
it split open to release hundreds upon hundreds of gold and silver mylar
balloons to gently drift down under the soft moonlight to thousands of
upreaching arms. And starry eyes.

Following Pages:
"CRACKED ACTOR": "CRACK, BABY, CRACK,
SHOW ME YOU'RE REAL"

LOOK BACK IN ANGER
BREAKING GLASS
SCAREY MONSTERS
REBEL REBEL
HEROES
WHAT IN THE WORLD
22mins
LIFE ON MARS
SORROW
GOLDEN YEARS
FASHION
LET'S DANCE
RED SAILS
4932 CHINA GIRL
WHITE LIGHT

BREAK

STATION TO STATION
CRACKED ACTOR
ASHES TO ASHES
SPACE ODDITY
YOUNG AMERICAN
CAT PEOPLE
T.V.C. 15
FAME

ROCK 'N' ROLL STAR
STAY
JEAN GENIE
2-52
CAN'T EXPLAIN
MODERN LOU

CHAPTER TWO

BAND CONTEST N

1) NAME 3 THINGS
   LARGER THAN NAVAL
   DENIS O'REAGANS
                    INSET NAVEL
   HEAD AS A CHILD

SET
NET   TONY'S GAS ONSET LEIN
LET
LEI
TAO
TOIL   1) the inflatable world
LIT   (HIS WILLY) + MY WILLY
SULTAN   2) several pineapples
INSOLE   (GUT)
TINSEL   3) Madison Square Garden
INSULATE NOEL EAST   4) LUST   SILT
                       5) MILTON BURN
                          (EVNIS BURN)

OUST   STEIN   OVULATE   SLAT   SALV
LIST   LANE
LOST   STAIN   LOUT   SALVE TIN
LOSE   LOUSE OUT.   SOLVE
        "SUAVE   INSULT SOIL
         NAUSEA   USE
         NAIVE   SLAIN AVIAN LINT   OV
                   NIT   IT'S

T HIS IS HOW A SHOW
goes: Sometime after midnight you check into the latest hotel after the
last flight and the last show and the last city and you discover that room
service has already shut down and your ubiquitous RCA 19-inch-Hotel-
Special TV is serving you either Inspirational-Messages-Concerned-
With-The-State-Of-Your-Soul *or* Crapola-Old-Movies-Interrupted-With-
Messages-Concerned-With-The-State-Of-Your-Wallet. In the
early hours you hear a faint rustle; the newsletter for the next day is
thrust under your door. That newsletter, impersonal and Xeroxed as it
is, dictates what you will do for the next 24 hours, when the next
newsletter appears. You cannot argue with it or cajole or plead or
dispute or fight or go to arbitration or wrestle it down and kick it in the
balls. *You must obey it.* It totally rules a major rock & roll tour.
Newsletter no. 65 for Monday, July 25, read as follows:

WAKE-UP CALL: 2:45 p.m. for band

BAGGAGE READY: not applicable

DEPART HOTEL: 3:45 p.m. for band, 4:30 for wardrobe/staff

SOUND CHECK: from 4:30 to 5:50 p.m. (doors at 6:45 p.m.)

VENUE: Madison Square Gdn; SHOW TIME: 8 p.m. approx

TRANSPORT ARRANGEMENTS: There is one bus for band at 3:45 p.m., there is
    one bus for staff and wardrobe at 4:30 p.m., there is one bus for
    staff at 7 p.m.

AFTER SHOW TRAVELING TO: Berkshire Place Hotel

AIRPORT TO HOTEL: N/A

ADDITIONAL ARRANGEMENTS: Please see the usual person by Thursday to
    change sterling.

That's all very matter-of-fact-style-rock-prole-prose for an emotional
peak of a tour with many such peaks. Hitting *"Venue:* Madison Sq Gdn"
is still the pinnacle of every major rock & roll tour, and for Serious
Moonlight, it was crucially important. Bowie had been away for more
than five years. In rock & roll lifecycles that could just as well be five
light-years; such are the verities of careers etched into polyvinyl-
chloride rather than granite. In point of fact, if you are a serious rock &
roller and you have world-class asperations, you had better be able to
handle the Garden or you had better hang up your rock & roll shoes and
go off to business school. The Garden has only 20,000 seats, but it's still
the measure against which all other gigs are examined. Get the Garden
or give it up.

Facing Page:
THE OFFICIAL TOUR LOGO, AS DESIGNED BY
MICK HAGGERTY AND DAVID

Preceeding Pages:
ACTRESS SHELLY DUVALL'S DRESSING-ROOM
PUZZLE IN TEXAS

No matter that the Serious Moonlight Tour had already torn up Europe and sliced through Canada and the U.S.'s East Coast: the Garden was the Big Hurdle. Quebec was easy, Montreal a piece of cake, Hartford so easy as to be hardly remembered. Philadelphia was memorable because Bowie was the first rock performer ever to do four sold-out nights in a row in the Spectrum's 16-year history. Also because—during "Space Oddity"—a large female fan completed the circuit break between audience and idol when she leapt from the balcony onto the back of stage right and swept by an astonished Dave LeBolt at his keyboards, eluded the bodyguards, bore down on Bowie in a rush, and caught him up in a sweaty, unbreakable clinch. He was playing his new red Ovation acoustic guitar for the first time and his panting pursuer got herself intertwined in his guitar strap so he couldn't take a step backward without pulling her along. Her weight finally smashed the guitar. Once she was finally pulled clear of the wreckage, Bowie made the best of things by deadpanning, "I want to apologize for my mother."

On the quiet, gray Sunday afternoon before the Garden onslaught in New York, the modestly-elegant-but-understated Berkshire Place Hotel on East 52 Street bore no signs of a rock & roll invasion. No fans crowding the marble, flower-choked lobby. No raucous musicians careening through Rendezvous Bar. No limousines stacked up out front. No rouged-and-mascaraed-and-leather-skirted-rock-&-roll-cookies lolling on the velvet couches and watching with eagle eye all elevators and doors for signs of The One and Only. That would come later.

Rock & roll moves in mysterious ways. Bowie may have been up in 1414, registered as "J. Rickett"—then again, he may have been secluded away in New Jersey or out on Long Island. Nobody's ever going to tell you just where he meditated the hours away before attacking New York with a rare intensity.

Up in suite 1114, on this sleepy afternoon, a meeting of part of the David Bowie band was underway. Even though most of the band members live in New York or nearby, they all decided to stay in the Berkshire for the duration of the Garden shows. The reason was, Carlos said, that once a tour gathers momentum, it's a bad idea to lose it. Very like a traveling sports team, they had become a team, and the spirit and camaraderie would be broken by any interruption. "You lose your purpose with days off," he said. "I'm glad we're working again. We're all tired from the time off. We stayed up till 5 this morning talking about how we all feel. It's roadshock. When 8 o'clock rolls around at night and you have nothing to do—no show—you have to suppress that adrenaline that's usually there. Then you get guys no good for anything but staring off into space. Staying on the road is the only cure for roadshock." Carlos, in a black bathrobe inscribed with his name, and Carmine, lounging in sweat pants and Fire Island Pines T-shirt were, together with Dave LeBolt and Steve Nutting, listening to a board tape (that is, one recorded through the sound mixing board at a concert) through a little Sony Pro Walkman cassette recorder/player blasting

RICA, WAYNE, JAMIE, AND GAIL IN THE PRODUCTION OFFICE

THE MIXING BOARD THAT CONTROLS THE
SOUND

☾

the sounds of "Station to Station" through four tiny Aiwa speakers.

"We do these band meetings in two shifts," Carlos explained above the roar. "Half the band at each. These board tapes are very, very precious. It's my ass if they get lost." This, a reference to proliferating bootleg tapes that Bowie fans are stacking up as the tour rolls on. He listens for a moment, then speaks up: "Hear that train sound Slick does on 'Station to Station'? That's not what you hear in the crowd. That's why we have these meetings. Otherwise, a musician might say, 'If they can't hear what I'm playing, then fuck it.' " Carlos laughed. "The tapes can lie. You're hearing these pushed through 1000 watts. But that doesn't count the crowd noise and the ambience of the hall." Dave LeBolt listens quietly to his keyboards in "Ashes to Ashes," then exclaims, "I don't remember doing that!"

Up in Suite 1610-1612, amidst sumptuous brown velvet sofas and bamboo sidechairs surrounding silver Serious Moonlight Tour file trunks, Bill Zysblat was, as was his custom, still in his brown bathrobe in mid-afternoon. In the tradition of 20-hours-a-day tour executives he was behaving exactly the way a rock & roll tour executive behaves. "I took yesterday off," he said, by way of an off-handed defense. Arnold Dunn, another veteran of the Stones tours, drifted in, still in his tennis whites. He and Zysblat conferred at length over who wants—and who actually needed—tickets for the Garden shows. They discussed when everyone should meet in Tokyo. They discussed the psychic properties of Eva, who had predicted a seaplane crash in New York harbor the very day before and had, in fact, warned off a Moonlight tour member from taking that very flight.

Down in the beige marble lobby of the Berkshire Place, Arnold and tour administrator Frankie Enfield are sitting on the overstuffed sofas as Frankie addresses Monday's newsletter. They're discussing, only half tongue-in-cheek, how to design a "quick-release guitar strap," so that Bowie could gain immediate freedom—should he ever again be faced with a Philadelphia-fan-guitar-grabber. Eva Strom strolls by with a handful of postcards that she displays proudly. "You can't buy these in England," she observes, very correctly. Members of the tour drift in.

It's 1 a.m. and all is quiet up in 1120, where Carlos is wearing a "Zippy—Nation of Pinheads" T-shirt and sipping a Miller Lite Beer. His little daughter Lea is curled up asleep on a camp bed in the corner of the room. Carlos is still trying to deal with the volume of phone calls from friends—real and imagined—that everyone even remotely connected with the tour was getting flooded with. Requests for tickets. For the Garden. Nowhere else would do. Another reason for the band moving into the Berkshire, Carlos noted wryly, was that it was harder for people to find them and demand tickets and backstage passes. "All these friends I never knew I had," he laughed.

It also helps that their hotels on the road are all first class and have 24-hour porters and switchboards—to handle tour demands—and other such little niceties. That lends an odd flavor to this top-of-the-line, state-of-the-art rock & roll tour: does effortless professionalism equate with a dilution of the original rag-tag rock & roll spirit? Or have some critics and observers mistaken crudity for integrity, amateurism for populism?

Note to self: what, if anything, does r&r stand for now?

Answer: a solid alternative to what is not rock & roll. Like Wayne Newton and James Watt. It doesn't even have to be that obvious and that crude for the answer to pop right out. Watch the crowd at a Serious Moonlight show as it flows and eddies at your feet, links from many generations joined together by chords common to all. Rock & roll is still a peer-group affirmation, a shared belief in certain values, a celebration of a certain personal freedom and joy. To say it is mere entertainment is to say that a space shuttle lift-off is a nice fireworks display. A major r&r tour is very like a political campaign, except that in this case the electorate woos the candidate and actually pays him to come around. Could a politician, as did Bowie, sell out the LA Forum in 90 minutes and then be sued—or threatened with suit, at last notice—by the California Angels baseball team for "disrupting" their ticket sales at mammoth Anaheim Stadium? Not too likely. A big-time r&r tour remains at its core an underground rail servicing many diverse stops in all corners of our society. And those stops remain a certain reaffirmation of some basic rock & roll verities. In "Let's Dance" I can hear the ghostly echo of Buddy Holly and any number of r&r pioneers who made these tracks self-evident. Anyway, you can dance any which way you want to. Ain't nobody can stop you.

At 3:45 p.m., a curious observer in the lobby of the Berkshire Place Hotel would have noticed—and remarked upon, as did several curious observers—several self-assured, slightly bored young men who, by their eclectic dress and demeanor, could have been only musicians. Musicians waiting for the van to take them to the soundcheck before the night's gig. Tony Thompson, the great drummer—if you drape a towel on his monitor speaker, it's gonna blow out at a 45° angle just because of the pure volume of his sound... I saw it happen—from the group Chic, was wearing jeans and a sleeveless Levi's jacket. He was draped in an overstuffed easy chair in a perfect version of the Musician's Slump—wherein you learn to endure endless periods of waiting by basically lying down in a chair so that you form a triangle, with the back of your neck against the back of the chair forming one triangle point and your feet planted firmly on the floor with your knees locked in a 90° angle completing the triangle and preventing you from sliding out of the chair if you doze off. Which is the whole rationale behind the Slump. Anyway, Tony looked up from his Slump and said howdy to keyboard player Dave LeBolt. Who assumed the Slump and said howdy back. They traded music business news: LeBolt had been on Billy Joel's HBO special the night before; Thompson had just been asked to play on a Peter Gabriel record session with Chic producer (and *Serious Moonlight* producer) Nile Rodgers producing. The other musicians drifted in. Earl Slick, as usual, delighted the curious

REHEARSAL IN VANCOUVER

87

observers with his outfit: blue suede elf boots, electric blue drape pants, white suspenders. Frank Simms's little daughter Molly was playing with her coloring books on the plush carpet. A heart-warming little rock & roll tableau.

At four o'clock, tour-meisters Frankie Enfield and Arnold Dunn packed the musicians into two nondescript vans and sent them off to the Garden. Carlos Alomar, as usual, was ebullient as the vans crawled through choked traffic down Fifth Avenue. "I can't wait," he said. "Time to get back to work. I can feel that adrenaline coming." The band's talk is desultory: a dirty joke or two, speculation about how long the soundcheck will take, predictions of how good—or bad—the backstage food will be. At the Garden, a cop waved the vans through a roadblock, and they drove slowly up the winding ramp tunnel. They were deposited five stories above ground level, into a world of cinder-block dressing rooms, equipment-packed corridors, and alert security guards. Out in the cavernous gloom of the hall itself, dozens of workers were scurrying about the bare concrete floor, setting up the red-cushioned folding chairs for "orchestra" seating and erecting a metal-pipe-and-plywood-barrier in front of the five-foot-high stage to discourage overenthusiastic fans from getting closer than they should to Bowie and Co. Behind the red chairs, the balloon crew was blowing up small—maybe a foot high—gold and silver crescent-shaped balloons and stuffing them into the belly of the giant, smiling, fifty-foot moon balloon lying limp on the concrete. Once it's full, it will be hoisted to the upper reaches of the Garden where it will bob gently. When Bowie races off stage after "Modern Love," his last encore, the balloon's giant velcro zipper will be triggered open—thousands of balloons will drift down onto the crowd.

There was still no electric power on stage and it was about three hours to showtime. Geoff Perren, one of the band's equipment handlers, laughed about the time as he hauled LeBolt's Memory Moog synthesizer up onto the stage. "This is the Garden," he said. "Everyone knows what it's like. But—it always gets done."

Out on the floor, Alan Branton and his crew were setting up the computers that control the lights and Steve Nutting and his crew were testing out the soundboard. In the production office, just down the hall, people came and went with great rapidity. The blackboard read: "Bowie Runners List: two cases 9 volt Duracell batteries, 30 bolts for lights."

Out at the main entrance to the Garden on Seventh Avenue, fans and scalpers were milling around in the usual pre-concert ritual. The ticket scalpers seemed to be more interested in buying than in selling—a sure sign of a sold-out show—and were quoting prices from $30 for nosebleed seats to $100 for the front row. "Bowie is money in the bank," a scalper told me.

PRE-SHOWTIME AT FRANKFURT'S FESTHALLE

THE WORKING MODEL OF THE STAGE FOR "SERIOUS MOONLIGHT"

THE WEIRD, PARTIALLY EXPLAINED STAGE CONE

Following Pages:
BLUEPRINT FOR A STAGE PRODUCTION

GROUND CONTROL AT ENGLAND'S MILTON KEYNES BOWL

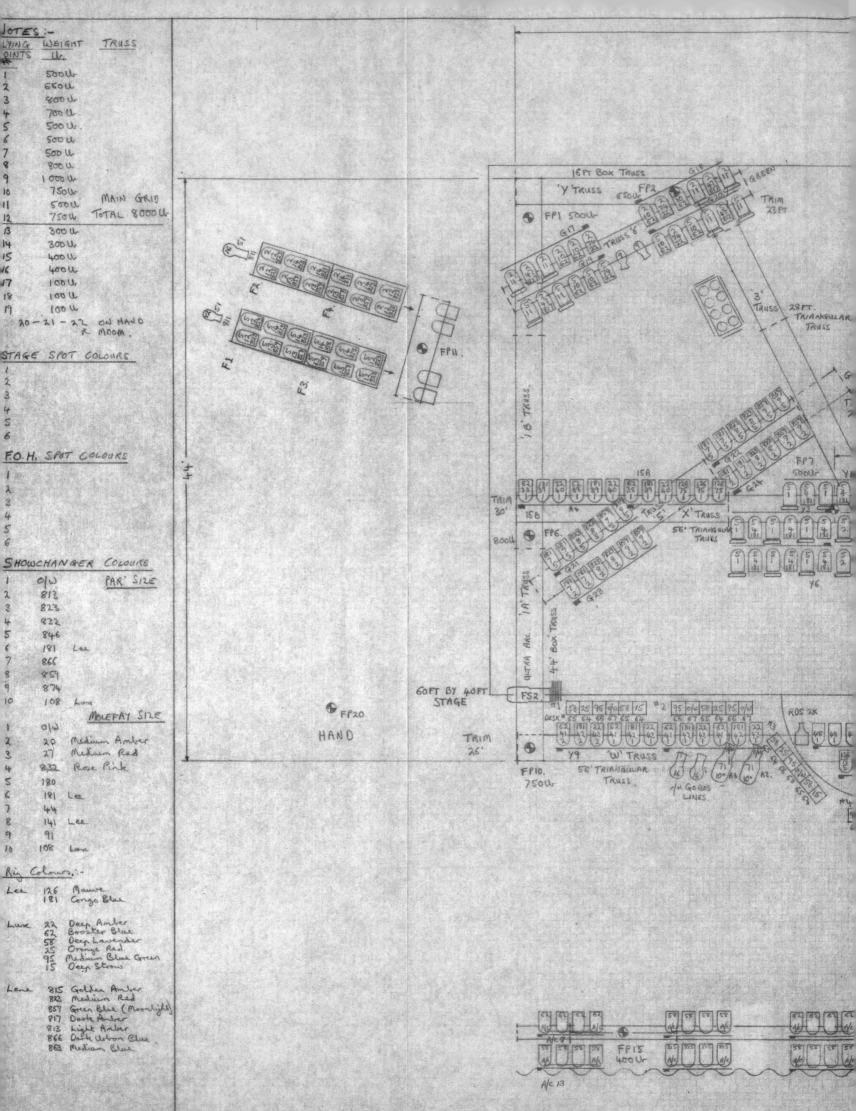

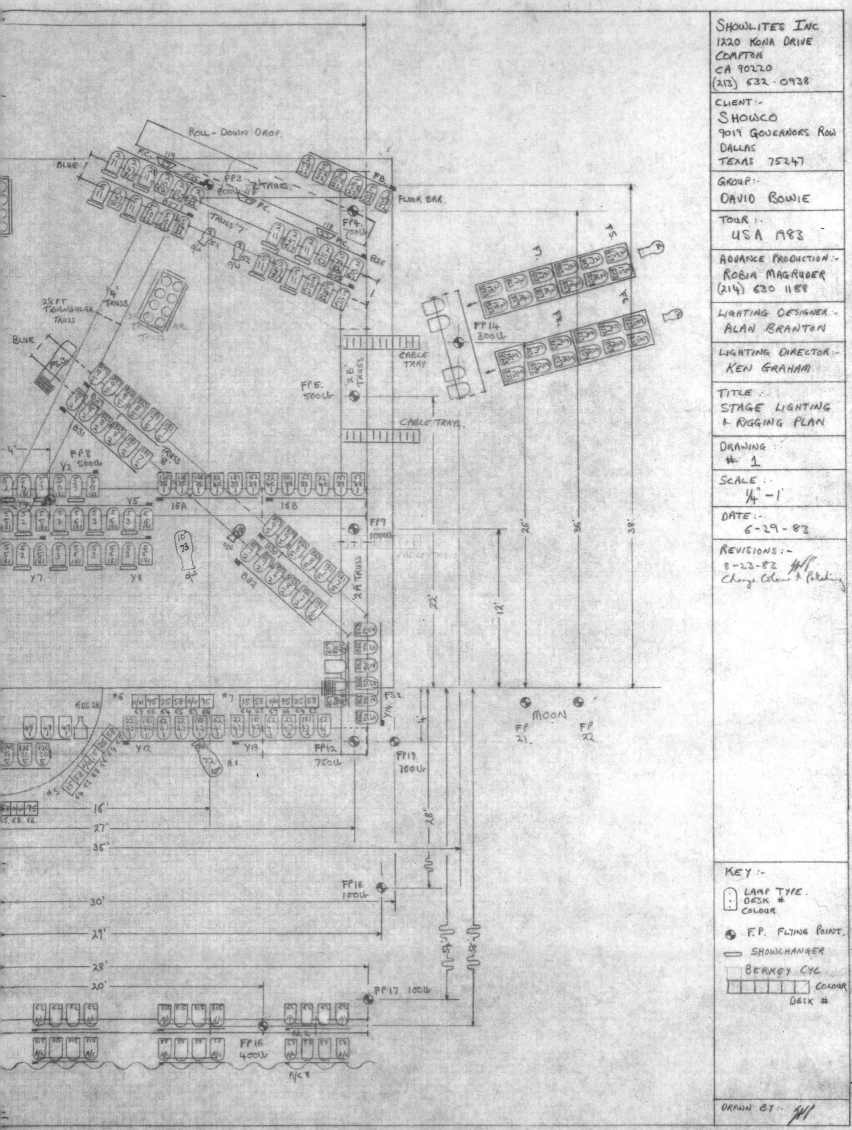

SHOWLITES INC
1220 KONA DRIVE
COMPTON
CA 90220
(213) 532-0938

CLIENT :-
SHOWCO
9019 GOVERNORS ROW
DALLAS
TEXAS 75247

GROUP :-
DAVID BOWIE

TOUR :-
USA 1983

ADVANCE PRODUCTION :-
ROBIN MAGRUDER
(214) 630 1158

LIGHTING DESIGNER :-
ALAN BRANTON

LIGHTING DIRECTOR :-
KEN GRAHAM

TITLE :
STAGE LIGHTING
& RIGGING PLAN

DRAWING :
1

SCALE :-
¼" – 1'

DATE :-
6-29-83

REVISIONS :-
8-23-83
Change Colour & Patching

KEY :-
LAMP TYPE.
DESK #
COLOUR

F.P. FLYING POINT.

SHOWCHANGER

BERKEY CYC.
COLOUR
DESK #

DRAWN BY :-

STAN HARRISON'S COSTUME AS DESIGNED BY PETER HALL

A BOWIE STAGE COSTUME DESIGN BY PETER HALL

Facing Page:
PETER HALL'S SKETCH FOR A BOWIE STAGE OUTFIT

Back in the production office, Frankie Enfield was carefully and methodically affixing the official tour seal to dozens of different sorts of backstage passes: laborer passes, photo passes, guest passes, press passes, doctor, promoter, loader, driver, caterer, security, stagehand, video, electrician, vendor—hundreds of people seem to be vitally important to the show.

Down the concrete tunnel, boxes of Williwear striped clothes were being delivered to Bowie's dressing room. To his amazement. He and George Simms, who is quite the linguist, were talking about which quick-language books they needed to get to prepare for the Japanese leg of the tour.

At 5:45, Carlos plugged in his Gibson onstage and ran off a few bone-rattling licks. Above him, some thirty feet above him, stage lights were still being wired onto the huge steel trusses. At his light control stand out in the middle of the floor, Alan Branton started testing his vari-lites and zapped the stage with dozens of winking, servo-motor-controlled rainbow-colored beams of light. Behind stage, Frank Pavlich was unpacking and tuning Slick's guitars. They're beautiful, simply designed but sleek. The solid black one has a black leather strap adorned with a red lightning bolt; the solid red one's strap is white, again with a red bolt. "These are DiMarzio guitars," Frank said. "They're custom made for Earl, solid wood, with 12 coats of acrylic paint." One of Frank's jobs during the show is to hover in the darkness at stage right with his equipment case and tools, ready to keep all the guitars tuned and ready to replace a broken string or broken anything instantly. The show must never be held up by equipment failure. "Earl gives me the red one only when it's out of tune or if he breaks a string. He likes the way the red looks in the lights. Carlos's little box guitar is like 21st-century technology. Earl likes an old-fashioned-looking guitar with modern hardware in it." David emerges from the tunnel for the 6 o'clock soundcheck. George Simms was singing "New York, New York, it's a hell of a town" through the sound system. Up on stage, Tony Thompson put on his golfing gloves and seated himself behind his impressive drum kit and twirled his sticks and then sent the bright sound from his Zildjian cymbals wafting skyward, all the way up to the "1939-1940 New York Rangers Stanley Cup" banner that hung from the rafters.

This is another hockey arena, as are most North American rock venues, but this is not just any hockey arena. This is, after all, the *Garden*. And the Bowie shows became special events, real rock happenings. And, since nothing much of real musical substance happens anywhere, much less in New York, Bowie at the Garden was genuine hot shit. And that always means that anybody who fancies anyself a hot property demands and demands again backstage passes for any hot shit show. Demands and expects them. Bowie told most of them to fuck off, redefining backstage passes to encompass only those

I'll stick with you baby for a thousand years
Nothing's gonna touch you in these Golden Years

☾
─────
98

persons who are genuinely working backstage and those few personages whom Bowie actually wanted to see. No more wholesale-meatrack-kiss-kiss-phonus-bolonus-receiving-lines of New York record label executives embracing junior executive weekend rock fans who were just discovering Bowie and starting to contemplate the possibility of matching a diamond-pierced ear with a traditional Paul Stuart or J. Press three-piece suit. They also, as hard-core rock fans who felt aged-enough and demanded to still be recognized as such, wanted to still be able to go backstage and mingle, just like you could back in the good old days of the Fillmores, West and East, when backstage wasn't plumped with extras and crazies. And one-shot movie stars.

Backstage at major rock shows became a synonym for crazy. Everybody wanted to be there and few were. Backstage in many ways defined the quality and the status of a rock & roll show. If no one wanted or tried to get backstage, then what you have is strictly a bush-league-amateur-night-yawner. If, on the other hand, you have fish-scale-eyed redheads wearing almost-stretched-to-the-limit-eye-popping-fishnet stockings and thigh-high-Three-Musketeer boots and an expectant expression and little else, lined up 12-deep at your backstage entrance—well, then, mister, you've got yourself a rock & roll show.

David Bowie had himself a rock & roll show. In the intricately wound concrete cloacae that are the backstage tunnels of the Garden, security guards huddled over complex charts that illustrate the many different backstage passes—that also changed from one day to the next. The guards thought and mulled over the many different degrees of access that each pass allowed: hospitality suite, backstage, behind backstage, and on and on. Backstage would-be crashers enviously eyed the portion of "Emil's Alley" (the tunnel where Bowie's dressing room was located; it is named after a former New York Rangers coach. Backward, George Simms noted, it spells "yella slime.") where thick blue curtains shut off from public view the real backstage action. The bystanders, who were performing their primary duty of standing by, were treated to the sight of a few real celebrities. Raquel Welch wore a dazzling white outfit that seemed to be a bit too small, though no one objected. Keith Richards and his lady Patti Hansen waltzed in like visiting royalty; tennis ace John McEnroe trailed along behind not unlike a lost puppy. Mike Nichols waved a hearty hello. Ron Wood was pounced on by the cops for trying to carry his fifth of Rebel Yell sour mash bourbon to his seat, and he finally settled the issue by stuffing the Rebel Yell into his pants before wandering out to his seat. Mick Jagger and main squeeze Jerry Hall came back to call on Bowie. Yoko Ono, Richard Gere, Grace Jones. Famous people to the left of you. Famous people to the right of you.

Famous people like to be seen with a winner, which is what Bowie is right now. What do you do with all these famous people, though? There had been maybe 7,000 urgent VIP ticket requests for the Garden shows hurled at the Serious Moonlight organization. Bowie's creative director Gail Davis sat up nights with ticket demands ankle deep on the floor of

Facing Page:
THIS IS THE TOUR'S DEBUT IN BRUSSELS

her apartment. How do you know it's really Lady Di calling up and demanding 20 tickets immediately? Is it politic to sit Warren Beatty beside Robert Evans? Heavy decisions, these. Plus, have you ever studied a Garden seating plan? The place is a mess, logistically. From the point of view of a ticket holder, the Garden is a vast upward spiral of lost hope. The seating plan, though, shows that it's actually a vast, hopeless, upward spiral, starting with Section 1, located on the stage level at approximately 6:35 if the Garden oval were a clock, and winding dizzily all the way up to Section 448, at 6:33 on the clock but perched way up in the oxygen-free rarefied stratosphere of the rafters. And then there are the suicide seats: the folding chairs lined up like firing squads directly in front of the stage where the hockey arena usually is. Very Serious Fans occupy these seats in sections ORACMJHEKJHG. So, where to put celebrity guests? You have to keep them out of harm's way, especially the older Hollywood types who might become cardiac casualties if some enthusiastic younger fan were to, say, accidentally spew a liter or so of Night Train wine all over the new cashmere jacket. What you do is take the heavies and lodge them in the loges—just above and to the left and right of the stage—and pray. The heaviest heavies—Yoko, Mick, Keith—you seat right up on the stage itself where Big Tony and Callahan can keep an eye on them. The 7,000 great unwashed should be able to take care of themselves. Here, though, is the way the Garden VIP seating list originally read: Monday: Robert Benton, section 36A [loge to stage left], row A, seats 3-4; Mike Nichols, 36D, A, 3-4; James Goldman, 36C, B, 3-4; David & Leslie Newman, 36C, B, 1-2; Martin Bregman—and on and on and on. You get the idea. Robert Evans, "Mick & Keef," Paul Newman, Dino DeLaurentis, Robert Altman, Lester Persky, Howard Koch, Gene Kirkwood, Richard Gere. The latter ended up standing in an aisle in front of several band wives/significant ladies, one of whom remarked rather frankly and loudly about Gere's height (or lack thereof). But few penetrated the blue curtain to Bowie's inner sanctum. The Rolling Stones did, since they were basically rock & roll royalty paying a state visit to an equal.

For the first time ever on a Bowie tour, Bowie allowed a hospitality room to be set up down the hall—well removed from his inner sanctum—where he paid a brief visit before the show to greet a few privileged VIPs and friends. Mainly rock & roll elite and movie industry heavyweights. The hospitality guest list was brief: Ron Wood, Paul Newman, Diller, Bernstein, Howard Gottfried, Dino DeLaurentis, Gene Kirkwood, Robert Evans, Howard Koch, Diane Sokolow from Warner Brothers, Gene Simmons of Kiss, Les Garland from MTV, Caroline Prutzman of EMI, Tina Turner, Mick, Keith, Grace Jones, Yoko Ono, Susan Sarandon, Dustin Hoffman, and the like. Woody Allen had been invited. Woody Allen's representative replied, Woody Allen "does not attend concerts."

He—Bowie—kept pretty much to himself except when special friends showed up. Otherwise, his dressing room was quiet. Glenis Daly

LET'S DANCE

Lyric and Music by BOWIE

did his makeup and combed his hair and checked his suit, and then he meditated and waited to go on. His dressing room—no better, no worse, than any other on this mega-tour—was about ten by fifteen feet. The beige cinder-block walls were camouflaged by temporary yellow curtains on metal racks. Glenis had already steam-ironed his six custom-fitted—by the Met, no less—suits and had laid out his Oxford cloth shirts and his striped regimental ties and his braces (not suspenders) and his shoes and hats. A table in the corner held fruit and cheese platters and *crudités*, along with a bottle of Louis Roederer Cristal Champagne (which went untouched).

Bowie, sporting a white silk jacket and little gold-rimmed rectangular Roger McGuinn glasses, popped into the band room, another cinder-block hockey dressing room, where everyone was sitting around talking about everything but the show that night. Meatballs sizzled on a steam table in the corner beside a table of cheeses and fruit and tubs of iced beer and Perrier and soda and juice. A coffeepot perked away beside bottles of Johnnie Walker and Stolichnya and brandy and red and white wines. Most of the wives/girlfriends drifted in and out. Frank Simms's daughter Molly and Slick's daughter Marita played tag behind the curtains. It was all very cozy and domestic; not entirely what everyone would expect of the rock & roll world. David sat down and read a review of the show and joked, "Well, I think this tour has legs now. It is a strong show. I can lean on it if I'm not feeling up. It's strong all around." Carlos had earlier said, seriously, "This band rehearses longer than most bands tour."

"Why is it so quiet tonight?" Bowie asked. "Is it just my imagination?"

"It's the union," Lenny Pickett told him seriously. "We can't talk."

Time dragged on. The last hour before a big show, after the sound-check, takes forever. Frank Enfield found out that David wanted to move "Red Sails" to follow "Let's Dance." "Now, how do I make 50 copies of a new song set in 10 minutes?" he asked himself, rhetorically. (The photocopied song list is taped on the floor or beside each of the musicians, equipment handlers, sound and light operators, and given to backstage security and staff.) The band donned their costumes and sat around like a strange touring troupe in a hockey dressing room: Dave LeBolt dressed like a coolie, Lenny Pickett like an Alpine mountain guide, Steve Elson like a Cossack, Stan Harrison sporting a safari rig, Carmine Rojas in Polynesian sari and yachting cap, Carlos Alomar a very dapper Nehru, the Simms brothers almost able to glow in the dark in their awning-stripe zoot suits and two-tone shoes, and Tony Thompson and Earl Slick looking pretty much like rock musicians. The three sax players—Steve, Lenny, and Stan—went off to practice their horns in the big, tiled shower room, because of its hard acoustics. Production manager Eric Barrett, an elegant Scotsman who was Jimi Hendrix's road manager, strolled through the doorway in his gray Serious Moonlight jumpsuit with the pink lettering (talk about

Following Pages:
WIT AND WISDOM OF THE WARDROBE
TRUNKS

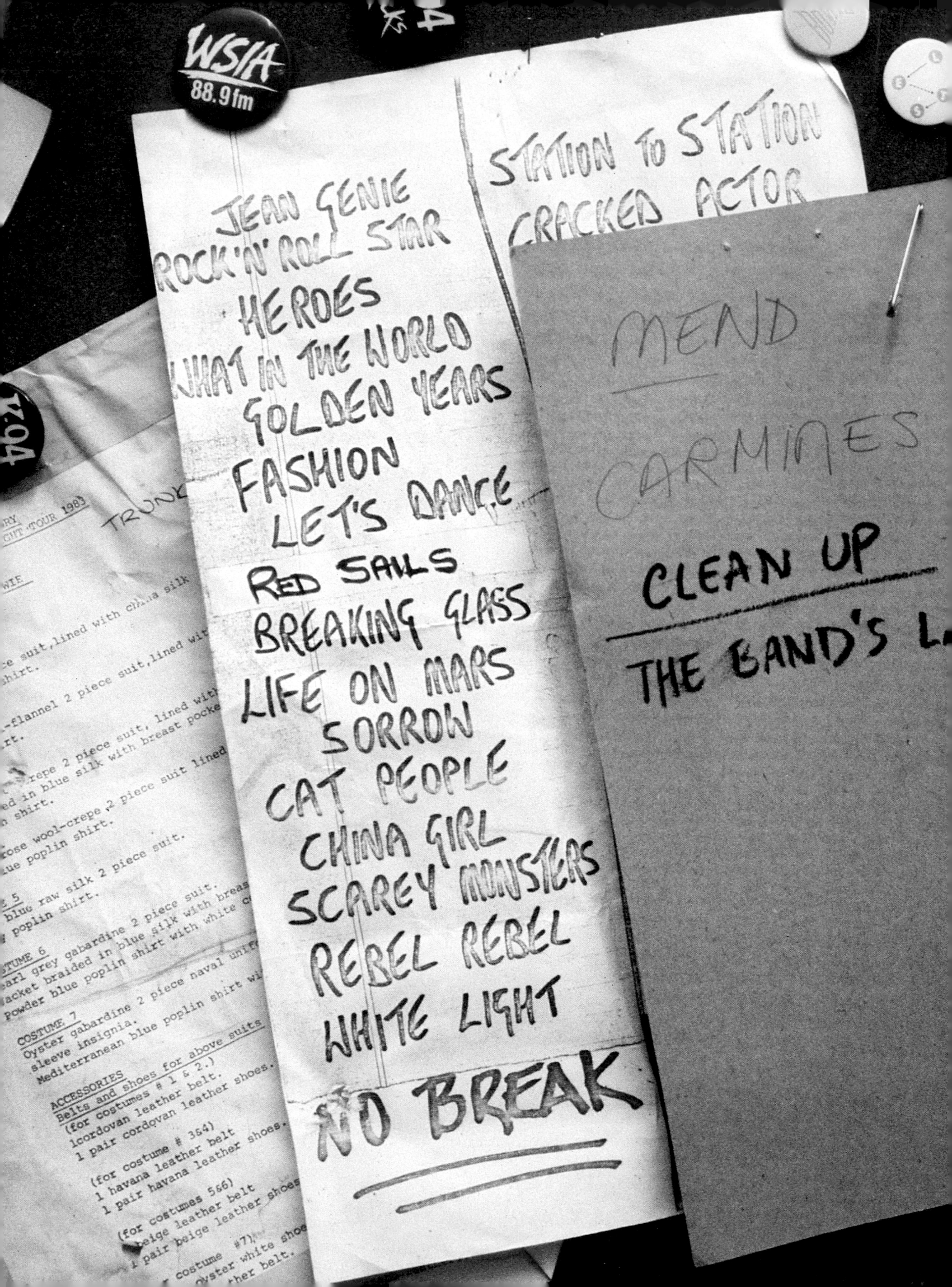

WSIA
88.9 fm

JEAN GENIE
ROCK 'N' ROLL STAR
HEROES
WHAT IN THE WORLD
GOLDEN YEARS
FASHION
LET'S DANCE
RED SAILS
BREAKING GLASS
LIFE ON MARS
SORROW
CAT PEOPLE
CHINA GIRL
SCAREY MONSTERS
REBEL REBEL
WHITE LIGHT
NO BREAK

STATION TO STATION
CRACKED ACTOR

MEND

CARMINES

CLEAN UP

THE BAND'S L

TRUNK

SERIAL TOUR 1983

BOWIE

e suit, lined with china silk
rt.

-flannel 2 piece suit, lined wit
rt.

crepe 2 piece suit, lined with
ed in blue silk with breast pocke
n shirt.

rose wool-crepe 2 piece suit lined
ue poplin shirt.

E 5
blue raw silk 2 piece suit.
poplin shirt.

STUME 6
earl grey gabardine 2 piece suit.
acket braided in blue silk with breas
Powder blue poplin shirt with white c

COSTUME 7
Oyster gabardine 2 piece naval unif
sleeve insignia.
Mediterranean blue poplin shirt wi

ACCESSORIES
Belts and shoes for above suits
(for costumes # 1 & 2.)
1cordovan leather belt.
1 pair cordovan leather shoes.

(for costume # 3&4)
1 havana leather belt
1 pair havana leather shoes.

(for costumes 5&6)
beige leather belt
1 pair beige leather shoes

costume #7)
oyster white shoe
her belt.

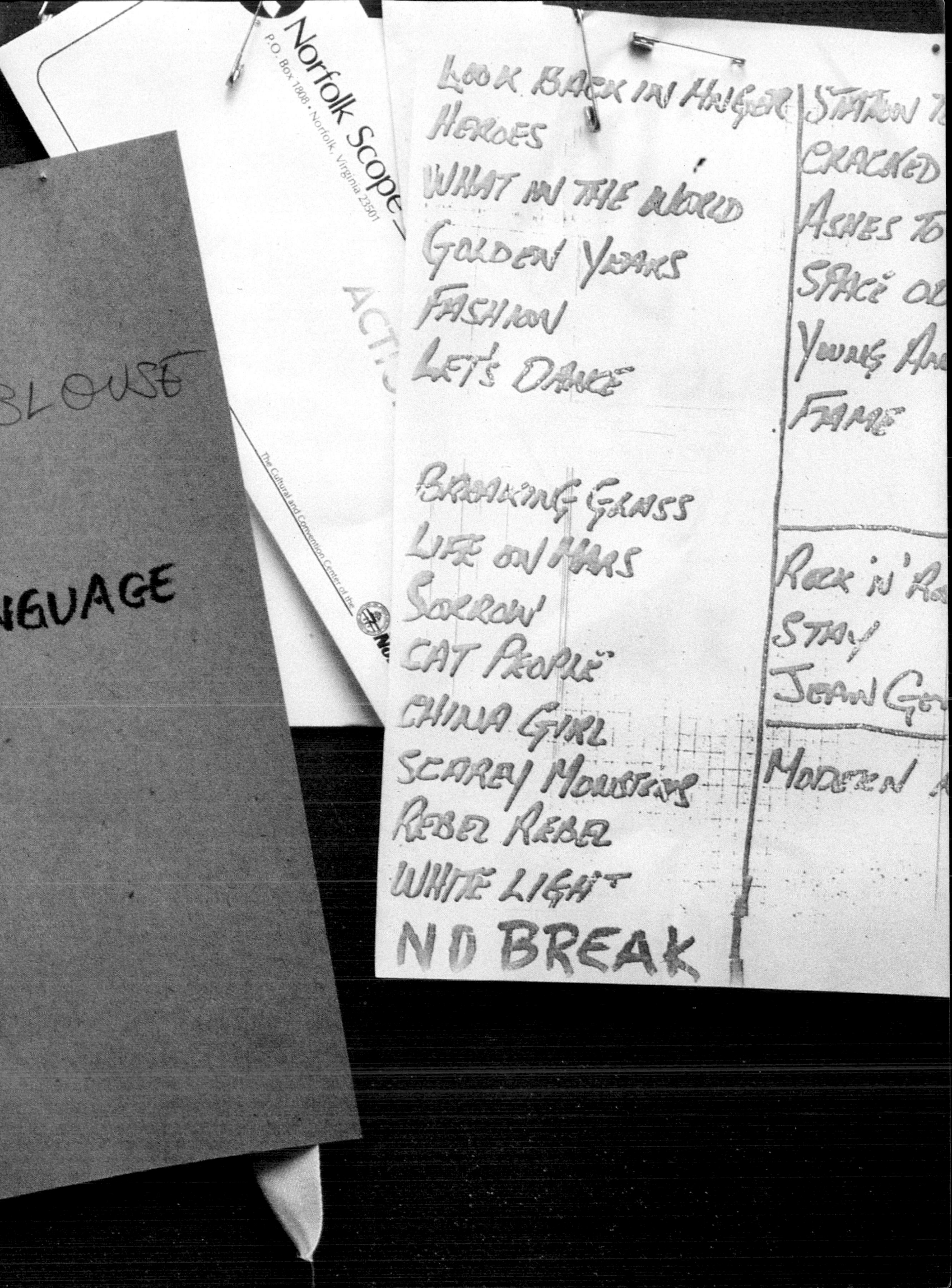

BLOUSE

NGUAGE

Norfolk Scope
P.O. Box 1808 • Norfolk, Virginia 23501
ACTI
The Cultural and Convention Center of the

LOOK BACK IN ANGER
HEROES
WHAT IN THE WORLD
GOLDEN YEARS
FASHION
LET'S DANCE

BREAKING GLASS
LIFE ON MARS
SORROW
CAT PEOPLE"
CHINA GIRL
SCARRY MONSTERS
REBEL REBEL
WHITE LIGHT
NO BREAK

STATION T
CRACKED
ASHES TO
SPACE O
YOUNG AM
FAME

ROCK 'N' R
STAY
JEAN GE

MODERN

FRANK AND GEORGE SIMMS, ONSTAGE,
HONG KONG

attention to detail: even the guitarists' fingerpicks on this tour are Bowiepink) and announced in his thick burr, "Ten minutes, gentlemen." The floor was already shaking from the crowd's impatience: 20,000 people stomping on the floor can cause a commotion. "Those are lovely jumpsuits," Susan Sarandon remarked in the tunnel. "Who do I have to, to, to, uh, uh, *uh*, to get one of those?" Barrett, his flashlight at the fore, led Bowie and band through the tunnels to backstage. They passed Big George at the ramp end of the tunnel. Big George is six feet, ten inches tall, possessed of innate dignity, and his presence at a New York City rock & roll event certifies that it's a genuine Big Deal Event. Big George shook Bowie's hand as he strode by Big George's checkpoint. "Have a good one," Big George rumbled.

The band, along with Coco and Callahan and Arnold and Frankie and Glenis and Robyn and Denis and Amy, assembled by a cluster of black Showco equipment trucks behind the tiny backstage area. The floor—solid concrete, five floors up from Seventh Avenue—was actually, physically, shaking from the crowd's stomping. As a sax tune floated out over the PA system, Carlos started bouncing up and down. "They're playing our song," he exulted.

The song, Bowie said, is "All Right, All Right" by Alan Freed. "That's probably Red Prysock on tenor," Bowie said as he puffed on a Marlboro while the crowd noise rose to ear-shattering levels. He has changed into his powder blue suit for his first New York show. He is probably the only rock superstar to wear his wristwatch on stage.

"Stand by, guys," shouted Barrett.

"Why does New York get everybody so uptight?" Bowie asked with a laugh that did not completely disguise the tension behind his question. "It's just another bar," he joked, as he paced before taking the stage. He laughed and ground out his cigarette and then raced up the steps to take the spotlight and the cheers and to command the stage and launch into "Rock and Roll Star." Meanwhile, back out on Seventh Avenue, the police captain in charge of the detail said that he had sixty men deployed, including mounted police officers, and that that was the usual number for a "major star."

Especially since the city was very nervous after a Diana Ross concert in Central Park only days before had sparked uncontrollable gang-robbings and general mayhem in the streets of Manhattan.

Nothing like that is going to happen in or around a David Bowie concert, at least not while there's still life and breath in promoter Ron Delsener, who was the first American promoter to have the faith to book Bowie (back in 1972 into Carnegie Hall). The New York *Times* review of that concert adroitly praised Bowie's sense of theatrics.

Advance stories about Bowie had most of us expecting a performance that would be little more than a transvestite fashion show with musical accompani-

BAND MEMBERS INCLUDED ON FACING PAGE,
CLOCKWISE; LENNY PICKETT, SAXOPHONE;
GUITARIST AND BAND LEADER CARLOS
ALOMAR; LEAD GUITARIST EARL SLICK;
CARLOS AGAIN; STEVE ELSON, SAXOPHONE;
STAN HARRISON, SAXOPHONE; AND DAVE
LE BOLT. KEYBOARDS. NOT PICTURED HERE
ARE DRUMMER TONY THOMPSON AND
BASSIST CARMINE ROJAS.

ment. But despite Bowie's obvious interest in unusual costuming, make-up and dyed hair, he is a solidly competent stage performer who brings a strong sense of professionalism to every move he makes. . . . He understands that theatricality has more to do with presence than with gimmickry, and that beautifully coordinated physical movements and well-planned music can reach an audience a lot quicker than aimless prancing and high-decibel electronics. In an age of publicity overkill, that alone has to be counted a major accomplishment.

This is one of the *Times*'s few bulls eye, flawless rock reviews. Hats off to Don Heckman, who wrote it.

Delsener is keeping an eagle eye on all facets of his Bowie concerts in the Garden. He's still a believer. Here he is, hand-carrying—while sporting his best white linen suit and puffing on what I hope was his best cigar—a special pasta dinner that his 72-year-old father cooked especially for Bowie. He hand-delivers it to Bowie's dressing room, which is a courtesy you might not detect in a worldwide quiz of leading promoters. Earlier, I had caught Delsener standing alone upstairs in the hall, with one white-tassel-loafered foot perched up on the rail of Gate 14, as he proudly surveyed his domain. He likes Bowie: "Twelve years ago I booked him into Carnegie Hall, and I had a hard time doing it—convincing them that he wasn't some kind of freak. David's great. His tickets here sold out in a couple of hours. I wish I could have gotten him to add even more nights [he did add one]. He could have broken Elton's record here, of seven nights. David's hot enough now."

In Band Room II, a backstage staging area, Mrs. Elson, Mrs. Slick, and Mrs. Simms chatted as Marita and Molly and Leah, Carlos's daughter, raced around the room and discovered the extra dimension of the possibilities of trashing a rock & roll dressing room . . . as a juvenile. Veteran rock & roller Ian Hunter—Bowie's old buddy and protégé for whom Bowie wrote the slightly warped teen anthem "All the Young Dudes," whose dudes carry their ludes (shorthand for Quaaludes, a drug, of course, a tranq meant for hopeless menties that became a sexual stimulant for deviates and others)—slumped himself down into a sling chair and through his Ray-Ban shades scanned the New York *Post* and tried to be cool and not notice the screaming little kids running around his ankles. It wasn't like this in the old days, back when Hunter was heading up the fine group Mott the Hoople. Rock & roll had finally matured, the appearances seemed to say. Had it?

Well, who's the authority? Who cuts the velvet ribbon and officially names the event and thus certifies it once and for all for history? No one. Not when it comes to rock & roll. Critics don't matter, self-proclaimed rock historians don't matter. TV crews from the evening news don't matter. No matter that Bowie was the cover of *Time*, the first *Time* rock cover since Springsteen. Audiences do the voting. With their bodies. Either they come to a show or they don't. They came to Bowie's shows. And they came from wildly different constituencies. A T-shirted-and-denim-clad army of teenies just discovering Bowie rumbled in on the subway. Fortyish liberals who had perhaps made their money

THIS *TIME* MAGAZINE COVER DESIGNED BY MICK HAGGERTY ON NEWSSTANDS JUST BEFORE THE AMERICAN LEG OF THE TOUR BEGAN

Facing Page:
GUITARIST EARL SLICK KNOWS-HOW TO WEAR A TATTOO

CARLOS AND CARMINE AT THE QUEBEC CITY REHEARSALS

CARLOS HANDLES THE GUITAR BREAK IN "GOLDEN YEARS"

by capitalizing on rock's counterculture left their Cadillac and Lincoln limos stacked up on Eighth Avenue and pranced into the Garden, carefully "dressed down" in starched-and-creased Calvin Klein or YSL designer jeans and "casual" silk shirts. Ordinary people who happened to like Bowie came as ordinary people always do: in whatever they happen to be wearing when it came time to leave for the show. One woman sported a Levi's jacket with an incredibly well-done Bowie portrait painted on the back. A few exotics came as David Bowie; as David Bowie in the different stages of his career, but mostly as the present-day blond, cheerful, natty swell.

They settled happily, expectantly, into their seats. A buzz of conversation between strangers animated the Garden, a happy sound not often heard at big rock shows anymore. No tension in the air whatsoever. Seemingly, no wine-and-reds freaks pissing on each other and on (otherwise) perfect strangers. A bit of what used to be called a community: people uniting because of a common, shared experience. Some spilled beer and slurred words and staggered steps to be sure, but by and large people were studying the program and scrutinizing the relatively bare stage and comparing it with—usually—Bowie's spectacular end-of-civilization-as-we-know-it-Diamond-Dogs-stage-set, with its bleak city-of-the-future that Bowie decimated. None of that here with this minimalist-proto-classical stage that was a study in gray and neutral. A nonintrusive, unimposing, passive quasi-world that made no statement of its own whatsoever. Its function was to echo or reinforce whatever role was imposed upon it by the players. And by the sound and lights that would determine its reality as perceived by the audience. By itself, it was just a flat gray horizontal surface flanked by a large pointing hand at stage right and a suspended crescent moon at stage left. Above were some three-dimensional (courtesy of *trompe l'oeil*) horizontal girders that visually performed two functions very cleverly. First, they closed off the usually unclosed rectangular box that a rock stage is and gave it what rock shows usually lack in terms of any sense of proscenium. Second, they hid most of the hideous tons of lighting and sound equipment suspended on huge trusses 30 feet or so above the stage. Closing the back of the stage and giving it the soaring vertical presence that rock sets usually omit were four circular, opaque tornadoes-at-rest that—before the lights transform them into malleable backgrounds—look exactly like four very large, very round shower curtains. "I call them the condoms," Bowie said. Whatever, they are unusual and effective.

Backstage, Bowie, in his powder blue suit, bounces gently on the balls of his feet after his band races onstage. "Have they all gone?" he asks Barrett in mock-Richard III tones. "The whole band? They left me?" He's in a semi-shadow formed by the curve of the balcony above. Up in that balcony, fans are leaning over and cheering him and giving him various messages and commands, not all of which can be reproduced here. Judy X, who claims to be 17 and to a practiced eye would register in at no more than 13, offers limitless delights to anyone, anyone at all down in that privileged crescent of backstage shadow who might be able to get her to meet Bowie, at the very least, and perhaps things might lead to a more meaningful turn. She is not alone. Remember Philadelphia, scene of the ultimate onstage fan-performer clinch? Some of the Philadelphia hard-core are repeaters at the Garden. It's always a pleasure, in traveling around the country, to encounter the same friendly faces. But some of these dedicated fans are getting a little too familiar. They clearly cannot get enough of Bowie. A gypsy army on the march that is, by God, going to be there every night draped over the barricade right at stage front with roses (de-thorned) ready to heave at David. They are, by God, there every night.

They chant along as George Simms, in his best circus-announcer-sonorous voice announces, "Ladies and gentlemen! (dramatic pause) On stage (pause) in New Yoo-oo-oork! (dramatic pause) for the first time in *five* years! (dramatic pause) DAVID BOWIE!" Amazingly thunderous, floor-shaking cheers and applause, that could not be exaggerated even by a press agent. Bowie is met with a gentle shower of red roses (de-thorned) as he sets foot on stage to do an abbreviated version of "Rock and Roll Star." His simple "Thank you" at the song's end sets off a fresh wave of flower-tossing and cheering. He smiles with genuine, undisguised delight. No more artifice for him; no more illusion. David Bowie has achieved what he set out to do. Then drummer Tony Thompson starts a powerful pow-pow beat on his tom-toms. The roaring audience can't be happier at the new (or at least "latest") Bowie. He's strutting confidently as he begins slowly caressing the words "Lavender blue, dilly, dilly, lavender green." He slowly and sensuously wraps his voice around the opening from the 1959 rock & roll hit, "Lavender Blue." "I'll be your king, dilly, dilly, you will be . . ." He doesn't finish the line. Dave LeBolt, at his keyboards, slams into the familiar opening chords of "Heroes." What a great sound: LeBolt's thundering notes shaking and rumbling the place like a minor earthquake would, audience cheers swirling around and up to the Garden's rafters, Tony Thompson's mighty drums and Carmine Rojas's gut-shaking bass notes kicking in with a roiling sound as bottom-heavy as you will ever hear at a rock show. Marching along with enormous weight—but also with such delicate grace that you could only compare it to a charging rhinoceros: enormous power under control. Bowie leans forward with clenched fists to finish off the "Lavender" introduction: "Now, I (dramatic pause), I would be king (pause and funky bass notes shaking the Garden) and you (pause) and you would be my queen" and then—off to the races as the front rows of fans practically melt in ecstasy. An unexpected jolt. An expected crowd cheer at the shock of recognition.

Bowie is riding the wave, totally in control, absolutely confident: right now, in the whole world, probably his only rival at complete crowd control would be Ronald Reagan. The dewy-eyed, prancing, swaying, women fans who press against each other and the plywood barrier that

113

TINA TURNER WITH RON WOOD AT THE
GARDEN

Preceding Pages:
MR. JAGGER AND MS. HALL CALL ON A
FRIEND IN MANHATTAN

separates them by only two feet from the guy—one David Bowie—that they seem to want to appreciate as much as one person can be physically and emotionally and psychically appreciated—if not enjoyed or devoured—are what you might consider as the Total Fan. Numerous interviews with these Truly True Followers reveal a not-so-astonishing revelation: David Bowie is a pop star with an enormous following and a mystique that seems to incite women to first of all want to challenge him about his so-called many-sexed past and then to want to take a very active part in his sexual present.

"David's incredibly sexy." I heard this quote from so many women, so many times (the first time I heard it, it seemed like good copy) that I almost started looking for the orange-haired transvestites lurking about to see what their version of all this might be. Well, they love him too. For the same reasons. Good music, good songs, good band, good stage show, no bullshit. Well, what more can you ask for, after all?

More de-thorned red roses tossed by women fans drop onto the stage at Bowie's feet. Is there a nationwide network that passes the word that de-thorned red roses are the only appropriate floral tribute that Bowie should be suffered to accept?

Bowie prances out onto the little half-circle runway of the stage that lets him enter the audience and where his feet can actually be touched. Hands reach for him—gently, because they could actually grab him if they wanted to—and voices beseech him and he leans to grasp palms and accept flowers—yes, de-thorned red roses—and what could have been a dangerous audience encounter is transformed into a moment when the stage barrier between entertainer and audience disappears. Bowie is as astonished by it as anyone.

"Heroes" might well be his greatest song. He wrote it after visiting a musing upon the Berlin Wall. No words on paper can convey the emotions of the song on stage. David sings, nay, shouts, "I—(dramatic pause as his eyes challenge the front rows) I can remember." The Simms brothers' soaring harmony punches in with an answering, drawn-out "remember," and the Simms brothers come up behind David and form a triangle with him and they even lock their arms into little sub-triangles. Bowie again: "Standing. (pause) Standing by the wall." Simmses: "By the waaalllll." "And the guards"—Bowie chokes on the "d" in guards—(pause) "the guards shot above our heads." Simmses kick in with a lilting "over ou-ur heads," and it rolls on with the saxes driving it like a locomotive winding down to Bowie's soft "Just for one day." Which is nothing but a false ending! A rock & roll mainstay! The cheers and applause roll forward through the smoke and haze and then Bowie brings it around again, signaling to Alomar with a subtle toss of the head. "We can be heroes." He sings, and the saxes come in with a hypnotic seesaw run that has the front rows bobbing and weaving like a boxing crowd up on its feet cheering a champion on. There is no drug rush in the world that can compare to that adrenaline rush that hits when a Madison Square Garden crowd erupts in a spontaneous ovation for a companion. There were plenty of tight, excited smiles being exchanged among those who were part of the David Bowie Serious Moonlight Tour. Tech crew, light crew, band itself, you name it. Bowie himself, as the cheers washed over him, stood frozen in the warm blue cone of a single spotlight.

RICHARD GERE WITH SUSAN SARANDON AT THE GARDEN

"Thank you. Good evening," Bowie said, with surprising warmth for him at a New York show. Alomar counted off a quick "1-2-3-4" and punctuated it with downward thrusts of his guitar neck to start "What in the World." The blue vari-lites mounted on both sides of stage front rotated in a furious, Gatling-gun crossfire that ambushed surprised sections of the crowd. The condom-like columns became chartreuse trans-luxed, the girders above were a soft purple, the band members upstage were bathed in a gentle pink. Suddenly, shocking orange vari-lites stabbed out of nowhere to pin Bowie in a rapid-shift fire. The columns faded to green. The stabbing vari-lites turned brilliant white and locked onto Carlos and Carmine as they flanked Bowie downstage; then the white varies swung ominously forward to make random sweeps of the front rows, isolating here and there in telling vignettes the fan who was weeping and the fan who seemed on the verge of a climax of some sort and the fan who was making a bootleg tape and the fan who was about to throw a rose and the fan who was about to throw a shoe and the fan who was about to throw a note and the fan who was about to throw underwear and the fan who was about to throw up. The white varies, very like aircraft landing lights, swung about and locked their blinding white cones of light on the front rows at song's end. Fans turned and examined each other as if all had suddenly been thrust into the lineup at the lock-up.

One of the joys of a brilliantly—as in intelligently—lit rock show like this is that the crowd gets drawn into it as lights play across the hall and extend the stage to the nether reaches. The stage is not necessarily just a tiny bright pearl at the far end of a big room. The performer is not just a strutting stick figure on that pearl. The audience member is not just an ugly-on-a-stick-personaless-consumer. How rewarding to see a bit of involvement, where theater's fourth wall (that, of course, being the one between the stage and the audience) is broken through, as much as a rock & roll show can break through it. The audience involvement is undeniable. Lights are down. When they come up, they invoke an intense burst of applause of fierce recognition (and perhaps identification): Bowie is sitting in a director's chair at stage left facing stage right. The two columns at stage right are blood red. This is for "Golden Years: nothing's going to touch you in these golden years." The girders above turn hot orange, like burning embers, and Carmine's ponderous bass chords start descending: a segue into "Fashion." The girders are pale purple and the columns are shimmering pink. The band becomes quite athletic, doing crosses and un-crosses that would have to be charted to be believed. Bowie, though, is inspired, weaving a dance

☾

117

MICK JAGGER AND JERRY HALL AND GRACE
JONES, NEW YORK

☾
118

that is clearly a clever parody of an MTV (supposed) tour-de-force, underneath vari-lites that shift from green to blue to orange hues. Carlos surges downstage for his guitar solo, and—even as he does so—Bowie starts a graceful backward dance of skillful boxing moves. His bobs and weaves and jabs and hooks parallel Carmine's bass dives into "Let's Dance." One of the best song segues of all time. The columns are now pale blue. Orange varies run random sweeps back and forth across the stage and then blink to brilliant white and then pulse to soft purple. One vari hits Bowie with soft green. A white spot lights up the crescent moon. When Bowie hits the part with "under the moonlight, the serious moonlight," he is isolated by a green vari, and the sax players turn orange for their solo. White sweeps over Bowie on his next chorus and Slick's brittle-like-an-icicle-guitar-break, and then orange and blue carry the song out.

Bowie gets a great cheer when he leans over to accept a bouquet of carnations (What!) from a dewy-eyed girl who is pressed up against the stage barricade. Coco leads Tina Turner up on stage to watch from the darkness behind a monitor speaker at stage right. Bowie whips off his jacket as he attacks "Sorrow," a large sweat stain growing on the back of his blue shirt. He's laughing to himself between songs, he's enjoying it so much. It's a supercharged show. He races through "Cat People" (biting off the words "putting out fire with gasoline") while strobe lights punch at him like relentless pursuers. Columns two and three behind him wink on and off in blinding white, while the band is an eerie phosphorescent from the ultra-violet lights, and the girders above are a soft pink. When David repeats the words "so long" at the end, he is lit in fiery red by the varies, and those lights and the blinding white strobes in the columns blink on and off in rapid sequence, keyed to each word. Light as sound, almost. Audience reaction is deafening. "China Girl" is a tease in the best sense of the word and in every way. It's every bit of the mime that Bowie learned from Lindsay Kemp and has improved on ever since. The columns and girders are a delicate, soft red; David is bathed in pale orange; emerald green lights zero in on the band members, who have set up two card games on stage for this Singapore saga. Lighting becomes more and more a major force of this concert, when two Super Trouper spotlights from the rafters and two pale blue houselights suddenly pick out David: with his back to the audience and doing the old self-embrace, arms reaching around and hands caressing his back. Cheers turned to squeals as he erotically grasped the microphone stand and slowly and gently slides down it. "Scarey Monsters" is a charge of adrenaline. Branton's "panic lights" do just that, sweeping and crossing the stage like air-raid sirens, stabs of violent beams meant to be alarming. The song is pushed by throbbing, bile green vari-lites. White spots at the rear of the stage throw five-story-high silhouettes of the Simms brothers crouching and weaving like monsters onto the far end of the hall. The vari-lites flash up to a blinding white and yellow for "Rebel Rebel." The washed-out lighting shows Bowie's face awash in sweat—but he's laughing: "Hey, rebel,

your face looks like shit!'' he shouts. Bowie's throwing only fastballs tonight, smokin' 'em in and dazzling the crowd. The lights flare up to a blinding white glow, and he runs through the Velvet Underground's ''White Light, White Heat,'' does a very convincing version of a singer being electrocuted by the microphone, and—after a great knee-drop—races offstage past an extremely healthy Tina Turner who had been up and doing moves you must see to believe. What a way to go to halftime.

Arnold and Frankie wait with flashlights at the bottom of the stage steps to guide Bowie through the darkness. When you have just spent an hour being bathed with untold thousands of candlepower of some of the most intense lighting this side of the Berlin Wall, seeing in the dark can be a problem.

While the band is still winding through a rave-up ending to ''White Heat'' (Slick finally getting a chance to do his Guitar Genius solo strut), Bowie disappears into his dressing room to towel off, put on his lime green suit, and get ready for the second half. When the band troops back, Ron Wood hugs Earl Slick and tells him, ''Hot show, good show!'' Molly Simms rushes to her father: ''Daddy! I saw you! I saw you!'' Down the tunnel, by the hospitality suite, two beefy New York cops have a headlock on a brawny young man in a torn T-shirt. They hustle him out a side door so fast his feet don't even touch the floor. He was incoherently intoxicated and charged backstage. He will try the same thing the next night, with the same result. Otherwise, there's very little trouble. Odd messages make their way backstage: the usual outraged notes from people denied entry to the hallowed tunnel, love letters, business proposals, requests for money, song requests, and tonight, one large envelope addressed to David with the following message boldly crayoned on the front: ''Hi, I'm the one your secretary Amy told you about, the one who paid the $135. Please open this.'' No one seemed very eager to.

Nile Rodgers, in a white suit, arrives to congratulate Bowie, who, towel around his neck, laughs, ''The show's terrible, it's rotten. The second night in Madison Square is always better.'' Rodgers is one of the few celebrities who, during the three nights, will make it past the hospitality suite to the coveted terrain behind the blue curtain. Outside the curtain, there's controlled chaos each night as the crowd of invitees to the hospitality room somehow multiplies. New York being what it is, and show business being what it is, and the glamor surrounding this show being what it is, it is a veritable disgrace if you are anybody at all in New York and cannot at least get into the tunnel. All manner of music and movie biz executives and former executives and future executives mill around Emil's Alley carrying their clear plastic cups of white wine spritzers and bumping against everybody in the world from show business's support group: radio, TV, magazines, newspapers, trade magazines, advertising, cable TV, tip-sheets, consulting firms, T-shirt and poster merchandisers, beer companies—you name it, it's here. The Bowie tour is a magnet. Nothing succeeds like success, and there's no

better example than backstage at the Garden, or for that matter, anywhere else on the tour. The prominent, the rich, the powerful, the glamorous, the successful, and the mere hustlers—they all turn up, sooner or later.

Eric sticks his head into the band room to announce, "Five minutes, lads!" A quick hit of beer and then Eric and Arnold lead them again through the shadowy concrete corridors to the stage. Once on stage, Bowie moves the set quickly: "Station to Station" flows into a theatrical "Cracked Actor," very like a three-minute parable of the fickle nature of fame and includes, of course, Bowie's famous Hamletesque address to a human skull. Great crowd pleaser. "Ashes to Ashes" follows, into a standing ovation for "Space Oddity." "Someone's got a birthday today," Bowie coyly intones, after "Young American." "Happy birthday!" (It was for Mick Jagger's 40th birthday. The next night, he dedicated the "Space Oddity" song to Sean Lennon.) Meanwhile, a stagehand rolls a large—almost three feet in diameter—beach ball of a balloon with a world map on it (the world at his feet, and all that)—upstage to Bowie, and he punts it out into the crowd, Super Troupers following it like Dick Tracy, as Bowie lights into "Young Americans." Nice clap-along song that Americans like. The globe is bounced around, like a volleyball, by the crowd. At other shows, it lasted quite a while, was even returned to the stage several times before finally exploding. Here, a zealous New York Bowie collector popped it straightway and stuffed the fragments into his pockets, to someday sell at auction. All manner of crap is being tossed up on stage and landing beside Bowie's feet; stuffed animals, scrolls with messages that shall go unread, flowers, room keys, intimate articles of clothing. Arms reach for him as he leans over the stage apron to start "Fame." Microphones protrude from the front rows: bootleg history is being made. Hand-written notes are thrust at him and thrown at him by wide-eyed young women who must be described as "striking." Good-looking, that is. One of them—a, uh, striking brunette sporting elbow-length white gloves and real pearls—had been seen leaning in heavily against the stage barrier and singing "T.V.C. 15" along with Bowie with a slightly disturbing look of puppylike devotion dripping from her eyes. She had almost collapsed from delirium when Bowie was signing the imaginary autographs during "Fame," and she appeared to achieve a significant emotion of some sort when he looked straight into her baby blues. Then he's off, running for backstage at 10:12 p.m. and out of her life forever, except for the encores. She doesn't know that what he is doing back in the concrete tunnel is wiping the sweat off with a towel that Glenis has waiting for him and taking a hurried drag off a Marlboro that Coco has waiting for him and taking a quick swig of a Budweiser that Arnold Dunn has waiting for him. The band is silent, exhausted, reaching for Evian water, Coors beer, Welch's Grape Juice, towels. David leans down to kiss Molly Simms. Then, as the floor is still shaking from the stomping for an encore, Eric Barrett sends the band racing back up the steps first—"Yo, guys, stand by," he shouts—and

121

Facing Page:
A NEW YORK TRIUMPH AT MADISON SQUARE GARDEN

ON STAGE AT MADISON SQUARE GARDEN

There's a brand new dance
But I don't know its name
That people from bad homes
Do again and again
It's big and it's bland
Full of tension and fear
They do it over there
But we don't do it here

FASHION

RAQUEL WELCH AT THE GARDEN

then David, who doesn't need a cue, throws down his Marlboro and grinds it under his heel and sprints up on stage for "Jean Genie." The striking brunette meanwhile, has dug into her kangaroo skin pocketbook to haul out her Braun electric lighter and proudly wave it overhead as the Garden takes on a warm glow from the thousands of matches and Bic lighters being held aloft in the traditional rock & roll signal for an encore.

Meanwhile, Bowie's Lincoln town car is warming up in the tunnel, and the vans for the band members and staff are right behind it, engines huffing away. Everyone backstage knows that Bowie will do "Jean Genie" as the first encore and "Modern Love" as the second (and last encore), and—no more than a minute after David Bowie leaves the stage (even as the thousands of silver mylar balloons drift down from the ceiling and as the cries for yet another encore reach up to that ceiling)—he will race into a car waiting ten feet from the stage steps and will then speed out of this building and out of sight. Frank and Arnold stand by backstage with their ever-trusty flashlights to hustle David into the Lincoln, which already contains Big Tony and Coco. David will, as he runs by, hand Frankie his fedora and his saxophone, which he was playing on "Modern Love." After the band finishes, a few seconds after Bowie's bolt, it's *sauve-qui-peut* as ten band members, led by Slick who is loping so fast he's almost parallel to the floor, leap into the vans. "The Vans Wait For No One" is one tour slogan that is strictly enforced. Five seconds late? Forget it. You've missed the van which means you've missed the chartered flight which means you can't make it to the next city for the next show which means...which means, you blew it, buster. Which means you *never* miss The Getaway. It's called, oddly enough, in rock & roll circles, "The Getaway," and it's a wonder no one thought of it sooner, especially back in the hysterical good old days when bands would linger backstage after a show and then try to forge their way through a mob. Municipal police departments love The Getaway. It eliminates half their work. With The Getaway, Bowie is gone before anybody can get out of the Garden. Even so, as the caravan winds down through the Garden's tunnels and finally hits Eighth Avenue, New York City mounted police stationed there have to hold back a respectable number of fans, who somehow know that this is the very time and place to catch David Bowie. That's respectable.

Back in the Garden, backstage, it was like a family reunion—minus the family. All the B-level celebrities finally got to get back into Emil's Alley and get a free drink. And they thought Bowie might show up at any minute.

During the show, things had gone along nicely at the fringes. Big George kept a hammerlock on the main Bowie pipeline backstage: nobody and nobody's brother got back there who didn't belong. Big Tony, in his bright blue slacks and canary yellow Bowie windbreaker and his cigarillo between clenched teeth, crouched behind Dave

LeBolt's keyboards at stage left, ready to protect Bowie. Callahan, who is such an old hand at this that he calls his business "Call-A-Hand," stalks backstage, turning his trained eyes onto would-be superstar-hangers-out-with. It's not that the Garden's security isn't trustworthy, but, after all, Callahan has run security for enough Rolling Stones and Who tours that he can glom onto every rock & roll fanatic in the world. They can't run a scam on him that hasn't already been tried on the best that there is. And he still has a good time. What the hey, rock & roll can still be fun, even into 1984.

JOHN MCENROE AT THE GARDEN

After the third triumphant night at the Garden, there was a party to celebrate it. David Bowie had gambled and rolled snake-eyes and emerged as the hottest thing since hula hoops. Or Frisbees. Or those cabbage patch things. Robert Palmer's concert review in the New York *Times* read like a paid advertisement. And Palmer is a tough critic who has also been a rock musician. "God bless Robert Palmer," a Bowie wife/significant other sighed with gratitude after reading his review. Many of those intimately involved with the tour were holding their collective breath until the *Times* made its pronouncement on Bowie, Version 83. The pronouncement? Palmer wrote that the show was "subtler, more ferocious, more moving and more dazzling—intellectually and sensually—than anything the art world's most celebrated performance artists have come up with.... As an evening of sound, light, and image, as Mr. Bowie's critical, conceptual gloss on his diverse body of work, and as visceral rock-and-roll, the show was practically flawless." No wonder that the phones went out of control at Bowie's various New York offices—at Isolar and ITG and Sound Advice Productions—and an invitation to his party could earn you five or six C notes ons the black market. Various quickie-rock-book-writers were lurking in the shadows because Bowie was now a Hot Item, and New York publishing houses were eager to spew out some Bowie books. Every Manhattan socialite called in IOUs to try to get into the Bowie bash. All the gossip columns worried away about it. Nervous social climbers agonized over being invited or not being invited. They were right to wring their hands and moan. Because most of them didn't get the invite.

After David's last show at the Garden—if we may backtrack a bit—his caravan safely reached the Berkshire Place. That hotel's security force stationed themselves in the lobby and refused to allow anyone on the elevators who was not registered at the hotel. Bowie fans, who of course immediately knew where Bowie was registered, flooded the hotel and turned its Rendezvous Bar into a royal and uproarious fling, while trying to either sneak upstairs or find out where the party was or—failing that—follow someone who was going to the party. Authentic Bowie partygoers had to sneak out after pretending they were something else.

The party was held at Café Seiyoken, a suitably unknown and

125

TALKING HEAD DAVID BYRNE AT MADISON
SQUARE GARDEN

fashionable joint in an out-of-the-way-neighborhood, down in Manhattan's warehouse district. The food for the party was indescribably trendy. This was the menu: kappa-maki (cucumber roll), tekka-maki (tuna roll), white fish roll, *crudités*, cream-cheese-with-chives sandwiches, fresh mozzarella cheese roll stuffed with basil and tomato, tea eggs garnished with chicken, liver mousse, open bar. Moon-shaped balloons adorned the ceiling. Big George hovered as a stabilizing influence. Here are some names invited to this exclusive bash: David Byrne (Talking Heads), Richard Gere, Lorne Michaels, Susan Sarandon, Dustin Hoffman, Mick Jagger, Yoko Ono, Billy Idol, Mike Nichols, Keith Richards, and Keith's son and father. At the party, Raquel Welch declared that Bowie was "the Fred Astaire of rock & roll." Mike Nichols said Bowie was "wonderful." Keith Richards ordered a fifth of Jack Daniels as his first drink. Andy Warhol didn't do anything too untoward. There were few gatecrashers. Overall, it was a pleasant affair, discreet, and Bowie actually talked with most of the guests, which is quite unusual at a rock & roll party for a superstar. Rock & roll in the Eighties is in the process of being redefined and may surprise a great many people after it is. Ten years ago, the standard was Truman Capote unsuccessfully trying to cover a Rolling Stones tour for *Rolling Stone* magazine, with Princess Lee Radziwell trailing along behind him, not especially comfortable and not particularly welcome. Rock and royalty and radical chic never really got into bed together, as it were. These days, one suspects, what personifies rock is the financial press chasing after a Bowie or a Michael Jackson.

Especially when a David Bowie can do an around-the-world-in-96-concerts-tour that starts in May in Brussels and winds through Europe and jumps to Canada and the U.S. and then to Japan, Australia, New Zealand, Singapore, Bangkok, and ends in December in Hong Kong and—along the way—sells 2,601,196 tickets. To paying customers.

That's how a show goes.

Facing Page:
THE CORRECT YELLOW TROUSERS TO WEAR
ANYWHERE

Rock Concert: David Bo

By ROBERT PALMER

THROUGHOUT his 15-year career as a rock performer, David Bowie has worked out new modes of presentation, won new converts, then challenged them, his older fans and his own sense of limits by confronting them with new work in a new mode.

Mr. Bowie doesn't just make albums and do tours. In fact, he doesn't tour much at all; his three sold-out performances at Madison Square Garden this week are his first here in more than five years. But wherever his work confronts us — in a video he's made, on a single or a new album, in a film or, ideally, when he is on stage fronting a rock band — Mr. Bowie does his best to take us by surprise. He doesn't just have a new sound or a new look, though he does always seem to have those. He has new ideas, new slants on the most effective ways to mix sound and image in live performance, and a new set of concepts to tie everything together.

●

Mr. Bowie's "Serious Moonlight" show consists of songs from many of his albums, but it is more properly a performance piece, a single, coherent, resourceful and at times virtuosically imaginative mixed-media work. It deserves that designation as much as an extended piece by Robert Ashley

world's most celebrated performa artists have come up with.

The tour began in Europe, and th were early reports of some mus roughness, as well as gossip about last-minute replacement of the l guitarist Stevie Ray Vaughan (played on Mr. Bowie's current album and single, "Let's Danc with an earlier Bowie band regu Earl Slick. But by the time Mr. Bo and his musicians opened at Madi Square Garden on Monday night, a few musical kinks remained to ironed out. The rhythm section of G mine Rojas (bass) and Tony Thor son (drums), hadn't yet found a c fortable tempo and groove for som Mr. Bowie's earlier songs, and th were occasional timing problems v a few of the more intricate arrar ments. But these were very mi blemishes. As an evening of sou light and image; as Mr. Bowie's c cal, conceptual gloss on his div body of work, and as visceral r and-roll, the show was practic flawless.

●

When a rock star has been around long as Mr. Bowie, it's easy to ch the easy options, to give an audie what one thinks it wants, to lavish enough imagination and care on song or an album or a show to get please the fans, keep money in bank.

But Mr. Bowie uses everythi

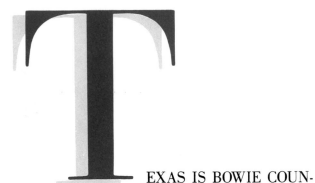

TEXAS IS BOWIE COUN-
try. Maybe it's because namesake Jim Bowie breathed his last breath for
this sovereign soil at the battle of the Alamo.

This particular Bowie contingent was relieved to be Texas-bound
after the pressure-cooker tension of Los Angeles and was glad to get
back out into "America" again. The LA Forum shows had been quite
intense, what with massive ice sculptures in David's dressing room and
a celebrity backstage list as long as your arm and Barbra Streisand
popping in backstage and every director and producer you ever heard of
and then some and even Michael Jackson and his four bodyguards
waiting—in the same tiled backstage dressing room with Cher and
Bette Midler—to be blessed, ever so briefly, by his Highness. LA was a
bit of an endurance test for all concerned. So the Bowie juggernaut
sailed on through its massive tour of America, with one brief stop en
route from LA to Texas. Phoenix had been added as a quick show—a
drop-in-play-it-and-fly-the-hell-out-again show. Then get the hell to a
luxury Texas hotel that understands and cares about the needs and
woes of a traveling band. A hotel that knows that the most important
thing in the world for a rock & roller may be something as simple as
24-hour room service or a pool and Jacuzzi and sauna available on
immediate demand. At any cost.

That's why the tour was doing a quick in-and-out show in Phoenix
and then skying into Texas to base there for a week. Departure from the
Westwood Marquis was set for 1 p.m. on Wednesday, August 17. I had to
buy a newspaper to see what day it was. There is literally no sense of
time or day or even place on a floating bubble of a tour like this. It's
either daytime or it's nighttime and you're either working or you aren't.
Cities are your benchmarks, your touchstone to reality. The weird
customs search, where they brought the dope-sniffing dogs out and
lined everybody up for a search? Let's see...that had to be Toronto.
When? Well, it was when we were leaving Toronto. Or was it Montreal?

Anyway, it certainly was Wednesday when we left LA. Bill Z., in his
tattered brown bathrobe, was on the phone up in suite 1013, getting the
latest weather and travel advisories from Captain Woody. He hangs up
the phone. "We're going into Dallas now instead of Houston. Woody
says Hurricane Alicia is about to hit Texas. The storm threat is too
great. So we'll base in Dallas now for the next six days." That meant

Facing Page:
"I'VE BEEN PUTTIN' OUT THE FIRE WITH
GASOLINE."

that Frankie and Arnold and advance person Eva Strom (who was already in Phoenix) had to do some fast telephoning to cancel all Houston reservations and find and confirm same in Dallas for 47 people, plus buses and trucks and cars and equipment and food and guitar strings and things. Glamorous work, this enormous change at the last moment. While the band straggles into the Marquis's lobby, Big Tony is out on the sidewalk puffing on a cigarillo, making sure there is no trouble, and sweating in the 96° heat. I tell him the paper says it will be at least 103 in Phoenix and almost as hot in Texas and humid as hell because of the hurricane. He snorts in disgust. In the lobby, Frankie is making a head count of the band and comes up one short. He gets on a house phone and then turns to announce: "Hey, guys, Carlos is still in the shower." At 1, the troupe boards a 40-passenger bus. "Well, kids," Bill Z. says cheerfully, "we're all going back to camp."

"Thanks, Uncle Bill," Slick says sarcastically. "Hey," Dave LeBolt pipes up, "this is the Zysbus. This is the same one we took to Palm Springs!" "Hey, Dave," says Steve Elson, "see if my gum is still under your seat." The bus finally pulls away at 1:20. Carmine is asleep; Bill Z. and Steve Elson discuss how to poach an egg properly; Glenis plans to meet her two children in Houston and worries about the hurricane; Frank Simms chatters away about Dusty Baker's steal of home plate in a Dodgers-Giants game; and Slick says, "It'll be great to get back out on the road and get some rest. My kid gets so excited that she doesn't sleep. And then *I* don't sleep." Arnold had gone ahead with all the luggage, and David had taken a car to the airport, along with Tony and Callahan and Coco. Finally, JET takes off from Imperial Terminal at 2:18. Captain Woody gets on the horn to announce that "we have a new masochist, a stewardess named Sherry, in the forward galley." He strolls back through the front cabin—with its 16 plush seats and TV—and through the big cabin—which has four sumptuous couches winding around a bar and a TV and a boomerang-shaped coffee table—and past the first spacious, wood-paneled bathroom. Then he sits down beside Bill Z. in the little U-shaped dining cabin, behind which is a TV cabin just ahead of the bedroom and its bathroom. "Bill," Woody says, "we're watching the hurricane carefully. It looks bad. What about your Houston show if Houston gets blown away?" Bill just shrugs: "We play anyway." One of the flight atendants gets on the horn to announce that lunch would be assorted quiche and broccoli. There are good-natured groans from every cabin. This is a lazy, sleepy flight with a comfortable air of camaraderie about it. Carlos walks by and stops to do his impersonation of Michael Jackson, which consists of pulling his hair down into little spitcurls on his forehead. David strolls by, spies a copy of *Newsweek*, picks it up, and reads its cover line aloud, theatrically: " 'Drugs on the Job.' Eh? What's all that?" he winks.

JET landed in Phoenix at 3:25 in a light rain, and it was off in minibuses to the Arizona Veterans Memorial Coliseum, a building that somehow brings to mind the word "heliotrope." As with most *colisée* around the country, it's in what is usually called a "down-scale area" or

BILL ZYSBLAT, JAMIE, GLENIS, ROBERYN AND AMY ON JET 24

ood in transition." No translation needed. This hall, built
t seems, seats 16,800; but it doesn't have room for the
drive inside, which is terrible for security, especially
y massing around the backstage parking area.
overhead, and there was a very real tension in
backstage were, to be kind, condescending at
enetic: either starved for rock or frantic for
all's doors opened at 6:30, there was a stampede
els and across the concrete floor for the best positions
stage: there are no seats on the basketball-court-sized area
directly in front of the stage. This is what promoters like to call "festival
seating." In Phoenix, there were no reserved seats at all. Fans swarmed
in front of the stage; others threw themselves prone across whole rows
of seats in the stands to save seats for their friends. Just behind the
fragile plywood barricade at stage front, Big Tony shook his head
worriedly. "This is how fights start," he said. And of course, they did.
Three feet away, a barefoot girl in cutoff jeans and halter top was
screaming at her rather fragile boyfriend, demanding that he defend
her honor by beating the shit out of a guy who was lying across the seats
where she wanted to sit. (He refused her. She left him. Third-rate
romance.) A young man named John managed to get a good seat: "We
got here at 4 o'clock. It was hell getting in; people were stepping all over
us. I love Bowie, though. I liked him first because of the visual thing. I
know that if it's Bowie, it'll be fabulous."

Security guards in front of the stage are stuffing their ears with
cotton balls. Phoenix was memorable because of the giant cockroaches.
At their best, dressing rooms—even in what we call major cities—are
inadequate. In a grim, tiled dressing room in a city that we shall assume
resembles Phoenix, the David Bowie band and David Bowie and son
Joey wandered around a steam table that made alarming, hissing noises
about the food that it allegedly harbored. This room, it must be
admitted, also contained a Playboy pinball machine and an Asteroids
videogame. Joey loved Asteroids. The room was brightened by the
presence of Shelly Duvall, a Bowie friend. Carlos had a headset plugged
into a Synsonics drum gizmo the size of a notebook and was happily
tapping away at it. Steve Elson and Lenny Pickett, on a couch in the
corner, were fixing a sax. Slick was asleep on another couch. Tour
administrator Timm Woolley labored away on his ledgers at a brightly
lit makeup table. Bill Z. worked away at the pinball machine. "This is
going to be one of those days," he tossed over his shoulder. "Nothing is
happening and nothing is going to happen." David came in, tried the
Synsonics for a while, patted the pinball machine ("Now, that's a real
game"), and then sat down to play Asteroids with Joey. At 7:45, Eric
poked his head in the door to announce: "Let's go lads! Thirty minutes!
Get made up, get into your silly suits." Tony Thompson just laughed
and poured himself a cup of coffee. Eric slapped him on the back: "Let's
go, black prince!" Tony, the power station of the band, said that onstage

"I can hear myself, Carmine, and some of the horns. That's it. I follow Carmine and watch David in case he ends a song early. And watch Carlos's cues. Yeah, my monitors are loud. I like it loud."

Out front, the place is packed and restless and there's a surprising number of blond would-be-Bowie-lookalikes. Backstage, before he races up the nine steps to the stage, David in his peach-colored suit, tells his band: "Everybody enjoy themselves tonight!" and his confident laughter is infectious and gets the band members prancing like athletes who can't wait to hit the field and kick some ass. A fast and loose night, it turns out. A hyper set by Bowie for a crowd that redirected its nervous energy from fighting each other to dancing. Dozens of tanned girls in cutoffs sitting and swaying on their boyfriends' shoulders. More of those damned de-thorned red roses hurled onto the stage. (Where do they get them? There must be a national hot line.) Shelly Duvall, in a crisp white pants outfit, perches neatly on an onstage equipment case. Her luggage is stacked in the band room: she will fly on JET back to her native Texas. The smell of popcorn in the hall is rapidly being replaced by the pungent aroma of marijuana. At the break, as the band rushes into the band room, Frank Simms says, breathlessly, "This is like Europe. I haven't seen a crowd this intense since then." Stan Harrison plays pinball. Steve and Carlos jump onto Asteroids. Eric announces: "Well, lads, you're doin' terrific. A bitchin' show, considering you're all on your last legs."

The second half is smoky and sweaty and raucous. Bowie turns the skull in "Cracked Actor" into a ventriloquist's dummy and bites it at the end. "You make a guy hot," he tells the crowd after a rave-up "Space Oddity," and he whips off his powder blue jacket. "I'd like to thank each and every one of you personally for coming tonight." And, of course, he started pointing at everyone he could see in the front rows and saying, "Thankyouthankyouthankyou." "Hey, you in the back rows," he shouted, "the show's started!" After he introduced the band, he said, "And I, of course, am Stevie Wonder." And during "Fame," he spat out the words: "Fame. Stick it!" It seemed like a musical cleansing and baptism after the LA shows. Or a reaffirmation of what had thrust him to the place where he now was. Oh, about the cockroaches. The Phoenix dressing room harbored insects that in some parts of this great country are called "palmetto bugs." You would immediately call them "giant cockroaches." They can fly. They are as big and as ugly and as disgusting as Roi-Tan cigar butts. Now, Joey was happy with his game machines. David Bowie was happy watching Joey being happy. Was it my duty to point out the giant *cucarachas* perched on the grimy concrete ceiling above father and son and steam table? Do you tell the star five minutes before he's due on stage that he and his son and his food are about to be buzz-bombed by the most disgusting bug alive? No, you don't. Fortunately, these cockroaches behaved themselves.

The Bowie mission lifted itself out of Arizona very late, jet-propelled for Dallas, the Big D. A BMW full of insistent fans wormed its way into

CARMINE AT A REFUELING STOP IN RENO

Following Pages:
VIDEO SHOOT OF "MODERN LOVE" AT PHILADELPHIA'S SPECTRUM

The Getaway caravan and almost caused an ugly scene at the airport. Bowie finally went over and signed their autographs and pressed the flesh and charmed them off the runway.

Then, at 4 in the a.m., the Bowie group is riding through the desolate moonscape outside Dallas, cruising across the craters illuminated by spectral moonlight toward the Mandalay Four Seasons Hotel, an unexpected vertical glass cigar that juts up suddenly out of flatlands. It is hard by an artificial lake and artificial canals filled with taxi-speedboats in an odd manmade city called Las Colinas. The imposed presence of this "city" is an uneasy truce rather like Bowie's music: a creative but palpable tension between technology and the earth. The band had spent 19 days in this remote—albeit luxurious—hotel during rehearsals. The reunion was not entirely joyous. Remote as the hotel is, security guards had to flush some zealous Bowie fans out of the verdant ferns in Apertif, the lobby bar.

The Dallas show is in the Reunion, a huge flying saucer of a hall planted firmly in downtown Big D. The dressing rooms are the best yet. The couches are so comfortable that you hate to get up out of them. The carpeting is so deep that a short musician might get lost in it. There's good food a-plenty and row upon row of Remy Martin and Chivas Regal and all the good stuff. The place is so well laid out that all you have to do to get on stage is leave the dressing room and run up seven steps. The only problem—so a roadie told me as he wrapped gaffer's tape around a rolled-up towel and proceeded to tape said towel to the concrete overhang that overhangs the seven-step run—is that said overhang is so low that you might scalp yourself in all the excitement. The Bowie band is sensitive to brainings: Tony Thompson ran off stage in Chicago and collided with a pole. The pole won. The band caught on.

Backstage, in the large driveway area of the hall, just inside the huge metal sliding doors, Bowie's band members were playing a pick-up game of basketball, and the cops and security guards and union stagehands were looking on with amusement. Joey Bowie, sporting a new 10-gallon hat that Big Tony had bought for him that day, was skateboarding on equipment skids. Bowie was watching the game. He was wearing a black beret and green jazz shoes and his usual trousers and safari shirt. He leaned against an equipment trunk and talked of how much he liked the energy and flow of Dallas. Especially its burgeoning skyline and how there seem to be no rules to its architecture and the seeming anti-architecture of Site's completely unconventional buildings and the new pink Mobil Oil structure. "The architects must have a wonderful time. And this place, the Reunion," he said, "it's a great, flat shape."

It's a slow night backstage in Dallas. Band and crew dine on prime rib, scalloped potatoes, squash, peas, carrots, and excellent banana pudding like your mother used to make. Carlos falls asleep on a couch in the band room and Tony Thompson figures—correctly—that depositing a pile of ice cubes on his crotch will bring Carlos around. To everyone's great amusement.

140

E.M.I. RECORDS SERVED UP THIS CAKE IN PHILADELPHIA

Preceding Pages:
AT THE SPECTRUM IN PHILADELPHIA

FRANK SIMMS IN YOKOHAMA

Shelley Duvall brought order and meaning to the band room when she marched up to the blackboard (this is, after all, another sports arena and sports coaches have to have blackboards) and chalked up the following: "Make as many words (three letters or more) out of this word: 'Evaluations.' Beat the all-time high of 235 words. Plurals don't count." There could not be a better tonic for a bored rock & roll band. "Is 'snot' a word?" asks Stan Harrison. "Sure," Shelley says, "we hear it every day." Then the band was off to the races—but not to 235 words.

Out front, the Dallas crowd is like the city itself: well-behaved, well-dressed, anxious to do the right thing and desperate to be considered hip. You never saw so many women in textured and patterned stockings in your life. Or as many men sporting white linen jackets. The fashion highlight is a young woman in a skirt slit high enough to reveal a raccoon tail dangling from what some people would call a knee ribbon and others would say was a garter belt. Such objects are flung at the stage and Bowie amazes everyone, especially his crew, when he snakes out his left hand and catches a fluttering red bandana without even looking. Naturally, this being Dallas—Texas—there are enough de-thorned red roses to choke a florist. Where do these *come* from?

Nothing happened that night, unless you are one of the clutch of rock fans who prowled the Mandalay's lobby, Bowie album in hand, and searched for the rock & rollers whom you thought should be raising hell, or *something*, instead of hiding upstairs listening to tapes or sleeping. It has been said before and will be said again that rock fans still expect herculean bouts of self-abuse by their rock idols: that every night of a grueling tour should be a spectacular Saturday night. That only worked for rock stars who are now described as "late," and this late doesn't mean tardy. The next day, the troupe left the Mandalay at 2:30 p.m. for the Austin show. Shelley Duvall showed her "The Boy Who Tried to Find the Shivers" Faerie Tale on a VCR on the plane. Exquisite shrimp and crab claws were served, along with carrot cake. As JET leaned down toward Austin's air space, Austin ground control asked: "Ground control to Major Tom. Can you hear me? Now you do the rest."

It's maybe a ten-minute drive to the hall, the Frank Erwin Performing Arts Center at the University of Texas. UT and Austin commonly call it the "Superdrum"—and for good reason. It looks exactly like an enormous concrete snare drum baking in the sun right by Interstate 35. These Sunbelt super-halls are stunning palaces compared to their crumbling counterparts in the North and East and even Europe. So spick-and-span and sparkling that "you could eat off the floor." Fortunately, back here in the spotless dressing rooms—full of the heady, spicy aroma wafting from Mexican food bubbling away in silver chafing dishes—you weren't expected to.

David was reclining in the band room on a couch that was so UT-orange-bright that you almost needed Ray-Bans to make him out, even though he was unmistakable in his green shoes, black trousers,

Facing Page:
HARTFORD WAS THE FIRST U.S. SHOW
AFTER CANADA

I will be king
And you
You will be queen
Though nothing will drive them away
We can be Heroes
Just for one day

HEROES

WRITTEN BY DAVID BOWIE AND INO COPYRIGHT © 1977 BY JONES MUSIC/FLEUR
MUSIC/E.G. MUSIC LTD./BMI

☾

154

Facing Page:
DAVID'S BRACES ON DISPLAY AT THE
MONTREAL FORUM

recommended Alan Branton to me for the lights. I think this is the first time they were used on the edge of the stage—"

So that you get the sort of horizontal cross-fire effect?

"Yeah. Alan and I felt the same way about having an asymmetrical grid as opposed to a straight-on grid where all the lights are on top. I wanted more of an empty feeling; a big batch of lights here and a few there, but not in the middle. So we had similar ideas of what we could do with lighting. So that it wouldn't look like just rock & roll. So we lit each number to the character of that song."

What about the costumes?

"The costuming thing was a parody, a slight parody on all the new romantics, these bands—" he laughed.

You mean all these new British bands that are called your "musical children"?

"Yeah. Quite funny. My musical children—oh God. I thought, well, it would be fun to dress everybody up in some kind of costume. I thought it might be nice to make it look a bit like Singapore in the Fifties. I had seen a musical called *Zoot Suit*, and I was very impressed by the clothes the actors wore. Then I went to see *La Bohème* at the Met. And I was equally impressed by those clothes. And, lo and behold, it was the same guy who designed them both: Peter Hall. So I tracked him down and he got very excited about the idea, because he'd never worked in the rock area. I said, can you just come and look at my band and see what characterizations you imagine and draw me up something? So he designed everyone's clothes. He saw Carlos as the Gandhi type, or actually more of a prince. His original drawings were brilliant. He chose all the materials and came to see how everything would look under our lighting. The thing with stage costumes is that they really look silly offstage. Like they'll fall apart. Put it onstage under lights and it looks good."

The word Alan used to describe the lighting that you agreed upon was "environmental."

"Yes. I described to Alan the feeling that I thought each song had. I think he's brilliant. Eric and I used to do all the lights before. And I had a fair idea of lighting, but nothing as sophisticated as Alan's, especially his knowledge of theater lighting. I was really proud, though, of what Eric and I did with white light on the '76 tour. That was quite a new concept and I've seen it used a lot since then. To have just different shades of white light, with maybe a little gold or amber gel on occasion just to change the whiteness. It was a great feeling. It was just trying to duplicate the old German expressionist movement in lighting. That was very successful."

How much thought do you put into the order of songs for each set? Sometimes it seems almost autobiographical.

TAPING OF THE HBO SPECIAL IN VANCOUVER

DAVID WITH HBO SPECIAL DIRECTOR DAVID MALLET IN VANCOUVER

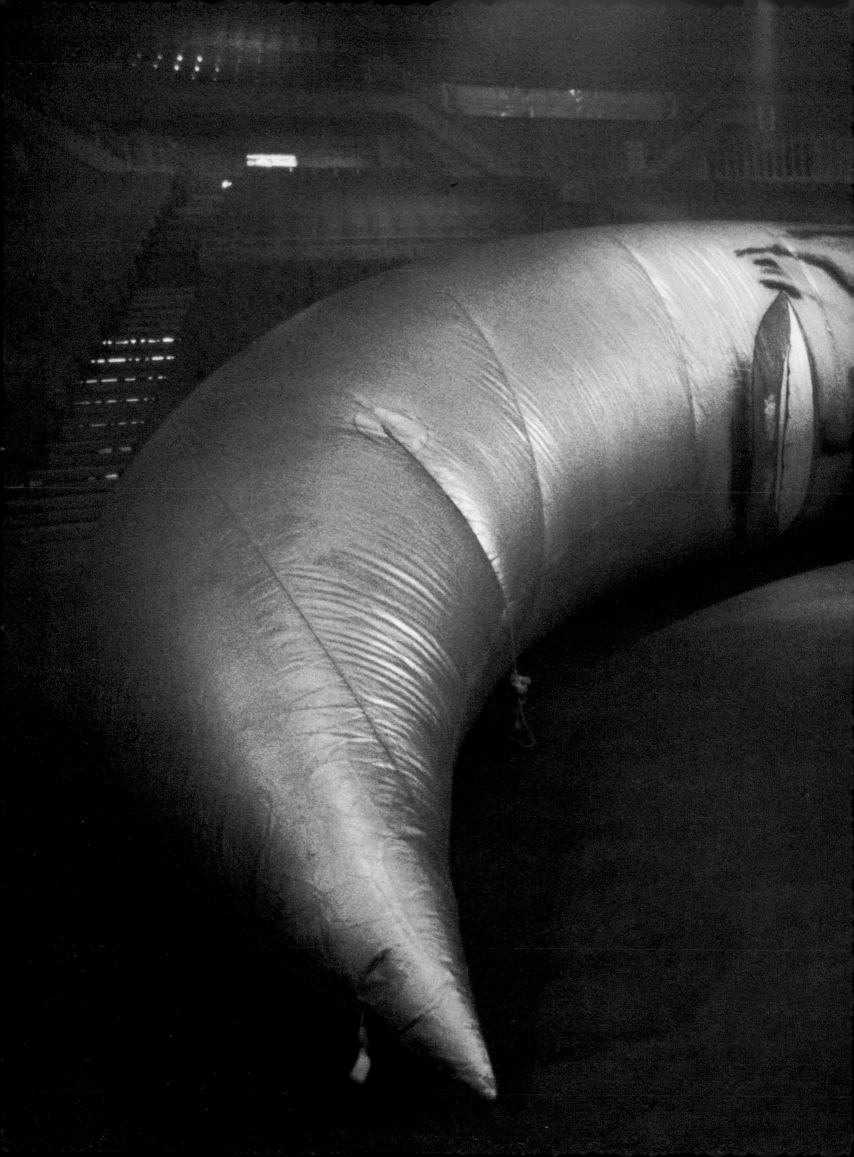

DAVID WITH MATE MICK RONSON IN
TORONTO

because right from the beginning Bill Z. told me we would be using DiamondVision screens for the open-air gigs, so it would be like TV and I thought that was great. So we did try to structure the show to work live and on camera. So you really get the best of both."

Is that why you were the only band ready to use the DiamondVision screen at the US Festival?

"Yeah. That's because I'd structured the show before that, knowing in advance we could use that. Might as well take advantage of it. It's wonderful." A satisfied laugh says so. "I like doing that. The three or four weeks of rehearsal are terrific. A lot of fun. Putting it all together and getting these guys to contribute as characters rather than just as musicians. And to relate and unbottle themselves. I mean, Lenny, I was trying to think of something for Lenny to do and he said, 'Well, I have this dance that I do.' I said, 'Oh, yeah, we'll see it.' And he did a whirling dervish...I said that is fantastic! Can I put it into the show somewhere? So I put it into 'Red Sails.' It was such an absurdist song anyway."

How do you go about structuring a tour like this during rehearsals? You hadn't even met some of the musicians till then.

"I just let them get on with the music first. And Carlos takes that in hand. Quite honestly, I get really frustrated and bored reteaching musicians the old songs all over again, and Carlos really takes the weight off my shoulders. I go to the early music rehearsals and the later music rehearsals. I don't tell the musicians anything about the shows. Never. 'Cause," he laughs, "it scares 'em. If I said it to some guy, 'You're gonna be dressed up as a Chinaman and you're gonna leap about the stage,' I might get a reply like, 'Hey, man, we're musicians. Oh no, don't lay that on me, please.' So I gradually bring them into it. I started videotaping rehearsals when we started doing movement and specific choreography. And then play the tapes back for the whole band to watch. They would start to understand what you can do onstage. What you think you're doing onstage and what the audience is actually seeing: those are two such different worlds. Video is great for teaching that. They got into it totally. And I haven't had to compromise anything."

So you build around a show rather than the usual vice versa?

"Right. I've got to build the band around the music. I mean, it's pointless trying to find character musicians, because they might not have the musicianship. So I go for the sound first. Once the sound's together, then I'll work with their characters. For this tour, I used a lot of guys who played on the album. Lenny came in afterwards because the lead tenor sax dropped out at the last minute. And Slick was late because of the young Mr. Stevie Ray Vaughan and his career." He laughs heartily.

Preceding Pages:
THE TOUR MOON WAITING TO RISE IN
VANCOUVER

THE SUSHI BAR BACKSTAGE AT THE VANCOUVER SHOW

BOWIE, CARLOS, AND CARMINE JUST HITTING THE GETAWAY

THIS IS THE TOUR STAFF AND CREW; SHOWN IN TORONTO

What happened there?

"That was most unbecoming to all of us. That was quite a shock. I was absolutely—God, I was so pissed off about it. That really pissed me off. It's not Stevie's fault. I think he's got a manager problem. What an extraordinary man his manager was. I couldn't believe him. He was a cartoon of a manager. I mean, he was really something else. I thought it was a cheap trick that he tried to pull on us, and I just wasn't gonna stand for it. There was no way I was gonna be kind of—almost blackmailed into that kind of situation. I thought that was a very desperate thing to do. So Slick came in and learned the show in four days. And he's really come out of it well. He's been received very well. Maybe I put too much emphasis on how I expected Stevie to be received. Tonight will be the telling concert [Austin being Stevie's home]—especially if the Stevie Ray Vaughan fan club shows up."

This is the first tour, I think, where you've flown. When did you get over the airplane phobia?

"I had put myself in a situation where I might have had to let somebody down. Iggy Pop was working in America back in '78, early '79. We had finished doing albums together, and he wanted me to play piano for him on his tour. I said I'd adore to. But he phoned me [in Scotland] from the States and said the first gig was in four days. I said a liner, a ship, would take me seven days to get to America. I said hold on a minute, let me have a think. I thought, well, I've got to take a plane. It's the only way I can get over there in time. So I thought, sod it. So I took a plane, and it was all right. I used to hyperventilate in just getting on a plane. And taking off would put me out. I used to faint. Frightened. I'd sweat and turn pale. I had really awful times with flying. So I just stopped flying. Couldn't do it anymore. And I wasted a lot of money as a result. Gigs had to be scheduled four and five days apart, so I could take a train. And getting back and forth from England to America was always on a ship and I'd have to wait for a ship to become available. So it was really a stupid thing to do. But I just couldn't beat it. So I finally said, sod it, I'm gonna lick this. 'Cause it's stupid, not being able to get anywhere. And so, it worked. It really worked. I've been flying ever since that flight. The fear has come back two or three times on this tour. I don't know why. I've got a great plane, great pilot. I know it's more dangerous to drive a car, but it's still something. I'm just not in control of the situation, I think that may be it. And I don't like that."

Does it surprise you that the bulk of the reviews of this tour are based on a surprise that you may be normal, after all?

"Yeah. Well, I must be honest. I mean, I really made a big effort to kind of come down to earth, so to speak, for this tour. It's—I mean, I am a good actor. And the characters I've presented in the past onstage, they worked. They worked a bit too bloody well."

People not realizing that you were acting?

HIJINKS WITH ARNOLD DUNN AT SLICK'S HOUSE IN LA

"That's the point. And I was really getting pissed off for being regarded as just a freak. You know, I am a good songwriter and a good entertainer and a good performer and I like acting. I thought, well, I've got to try, I've just got to beat this whole thing, because otherwise it's going to follow me for the rest of my life. And I don't want that. I don't want to be all that stuff. While it was fun at the time—well, some of it wasn't fun. But I thought, that's it. I can't fight this stuff. So, if I'm gonna go back on the road, I'd better go back with a different principle in mind. Otherwise, I'm just gonna get stuck with all that stuff again. And it would just finish off my touring days. I'm not gonna be able to take it. I'm gonna dive straight back down again, just be an alcoholic wreck, because I know what it does to me. I just didn't want that to happen again, so I had to come up and come clean, you know. And just sort of say, well, here I am, you know. The show will still be entertaining. I promise you it won't be a cheap shot show. I won't be trying to put on any pose or stance. You won't see Mr. Iceman Cometh or weird Ziggy or whatever. I was just gonna be me, having a good time, as best as I can. And it's working. It's working. It's great. It's terrific! It's given me a whole new audience. It's given me people who, before, would have said, oh, he's that red-haired faggot, you know, we don't want that, we can't see that creep. Now it's changing. Now, they like it. That's terrific. That was my premise for this tour: to re-represent myself."

Is this what might be called adult rock? Or rock of the Eighties?

"I haven't got a clue. I don't know. It's just songs. I mean, what would you call the Stones' music? I'm only a few years behind them now in terms of longevity or whatever. And all I call the Stones is bloody good music. I couldn't give it a name. I don't believe all that stuff about techno-rock and all that. I mean, Kraftwerk were doing it years before I did. It's nothing to do with me. I like using all kinds of music that I'm inspired by. Let's not kid ourselves that this techno-rock thing is new."

What about all the articles that call you the leader and precursor of all this new music?

"I never, ever wanted to be regarded as the leader or the forefront of any movement. Ever. Never wanted it. I did want to be regarded as an individualist. But that's about it. And I never wanted to be trapped into a particular kind of music, or perceived as presenting a kind of music. That's why my music goes backwards and forwards, from rhythm & blues to tech-rock, or whatever. Because I never wanted to be pinned down. I'm wary about this, because I am not the leader of any school of rock. I've always been an entertainer, but that's not a school, that's just a new way of doing songs. The way that I've always performed them, which is with a great emphasis on their visual aspect. That's not leading a new kind of anything. That's just the theatrical rock."

But some still see you as the pied piper of new

168

Facing Page:
EARL SLICK IN PALM SPRINGS

TONY THOMPSON AND CARMINE WITH
IRENE CARA IN LA

STING AND TRUDY IN ANAHEIM

170

Facing Page Above:
ANAHEIM STADIUM

Facing Page Below:
BOSTON IN THE RAIN

That was where you had to come and go from the hotel through the kitchen door to avoid the crowds?

"That's right. And I still do that a bit. This has never happened to me before on tours, where just trying to go out has really become a problem. I've never had that before. In the old days, I could just go out in the streets with the guys and shop and stuff or go to the pictures. That is really a downer now. And now it's gotten to a point where I don't even want to bother. I have to ignore invitations. People will say, why don't you come with us? I say, I don't think I'll go. Because I know what will happen within 10 or 15 minutes. I just don't need that; it's aggravating."

How do you spend the time in your hotel room?

"I must have read more than I've ever read in my life. I've got half a suitcase full of books, most of them collected en route. I'll go down to the foyer in the hotel, you know, and buy a book, those paperbacks and stuff. I'm not even trying for good material. The latest one shows what frame of mind I'm in. The one I'm reading at the moment is about how the end of the world will come and how you will die. It's a straightforward account of what destruction is like with a megaton bomb. It's frightening. My God, this thing is more than unsettling. But that's the latest thing I'm reading. I hope it doesn't take me back to gloom and doom. Hiya, Joe." His son Joey walks in carrying a board game called 21 Baker Street. "I'll come in and play that game in a minute, son. You know, they sold that house, brick by brick, even though it doesn't exist? I think they took the house that would have been next door on Baker Street and sold it brick by brick and made a fortune."

When you played Berlin, did you go back and see your old apartment there?

"Yeah, we went back and had a look. And it made me very nostalgic. I had such good times there; some very bad times as well. It was good to see all that again. The people seemed to be exactly the same. I didn't dare go up. I didn't actually go to the apartment myself. I felt that would have been wrong. It was a Sunday morning and it was so quiet. I immediately wanted to move back in again. I do so like it in that town. And I'm not really taken with any other towns in Germany. There's something about Berlin, though, such a cross-culture atmosphere. There's so many different kinds of people and different kinds of culture. I'm a complete coffee drinker. I mean, I can sit in a Berlin sidewalk cafe and just watch people for hour after hour and drink coffee. And it's perfect."

What's your routine like on tour? Do you fall into a schedule? How does it go?

"The daily newsletter is the only structure. I mean, that's it. But, I just play the day by how it comes along. I guess a good hour or two is spent with Coco at some point, going through everything that's come

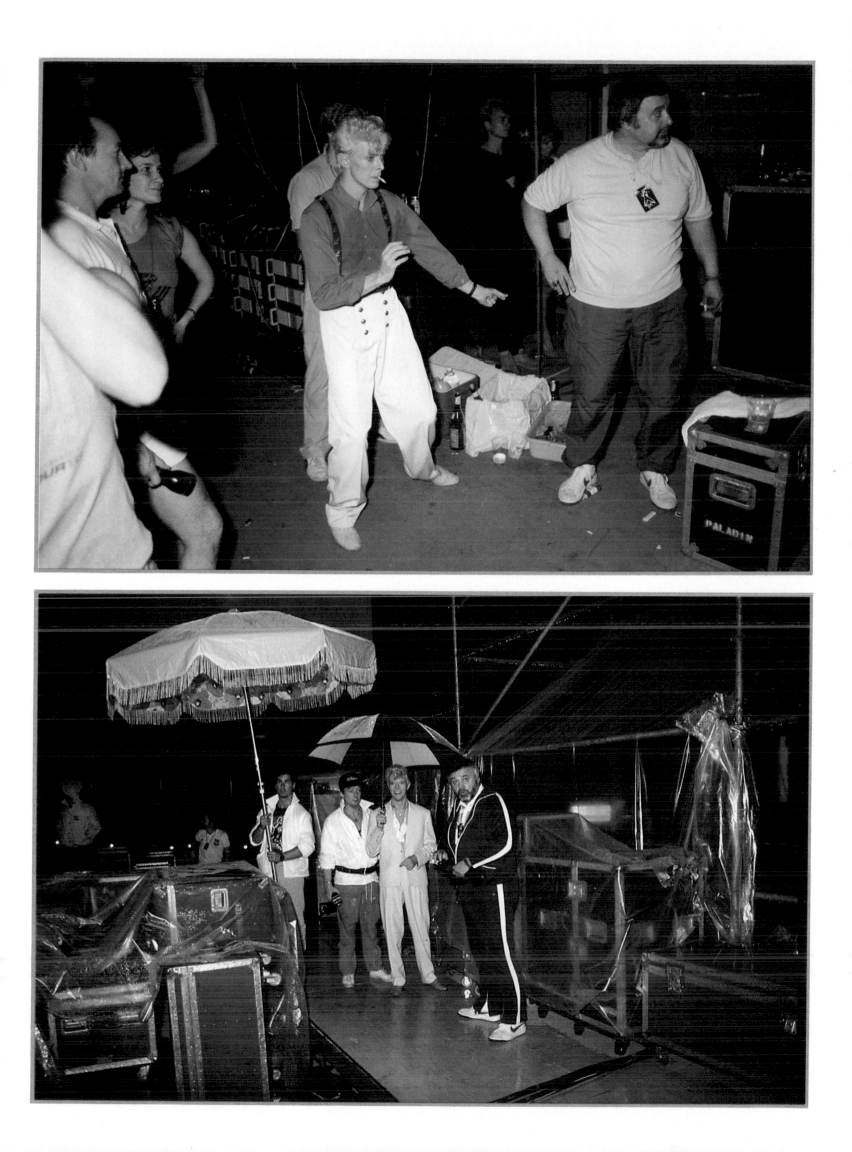

BETTE, CHER, AND MICHAEL CALL ON DAVID IN LA

DAVID WITH DURAN DURAN

GIORGIO MORODER WITH DAVID AT THE FORUM, LA

DAVID HEMMINGS VISITING DAVID BOWIE IN LA

WAYNE FORTE WITH MISSING PERSONS IN LA   SHELLEY DUVALL WITH DAVID ON JET 24 IN PHOENIX

IGGY POP AT ANAHEIM

up in the office. She tells me everything that I've got coming up this week and what I've got after the tour. I still try as much as I possibly can to keep my eye on every one of the affairs that goes through my office."

How did the Madame Tussaud's Wax Museum offer come about?

"They just called up and asked me to do it. I liked everything about it. It's a lot of fun. And I'd like to know when I get melted down and who I'm made into. You don't stay in there forever, you know. They turn them. I think they just turned Crippen, who was a mass murderer in England, into George Orwell, next to whom I am standing. I thought that was great. I was really pleased. I was quite happy about that position. I thought they'd put me in a rock section or something. I went in half-wondering—since they're sort of adults who run the place—if they expected me to turn up with red hair and everything. I was thinking, please God, don't let them put a red wig on me."

And you and Elvis and the Beatles are the only rockers there?

"I believe so. It's really something. I must say that the Elvis one is kind of weird. It doesn't look quite right. I guess it must be hard to work just from photographs. The Beatles one is pretty good. The ones that appeal to me are Burke and Haire, the body snatchers, who are down in the chamber of horrors. That section appeals to me. And Crippen, the one who was melted down into George Orwell. Crippen was in there with all his women behind the wallpaper. He used to wallpaper them up and drag them out every now and then. Really, really weird, man. I used to go there all the time when I was a kid, so this was quite fun for me. So now I definitely want to be a waxwork. How are you enjoying the tour?"

Tough to work, given the schedule, don't you think?

"I'm finding that very frustrating as well. I've got that guitar with me all the time, and I've tried quite a few times to get something going...."

The difficulty is continuity, isn't it, because you always have an interruption?

"Yeah, even if I've got a good hour or two, it's just that—nothing happens. I'm really finding it difficult on the road. I like to be with my machines and things. I'm not much good at just being the guy with the guitar and the tape recorder who suddenly says: here comes another one! It just doesn't happen to me like that. I like to sort of play around and do a bit of multitracking and things like that."

There don't seem to be as many Bowie clones lurking about on this tour as before.

"Yeah. The best one—this is something I just remembered the other night when we worked with the Tubes and they reminded me of it. This Bowie clone was living the life of Riley in Hollywood, hundred-dollar

Facing Page Above:
COCO SCHWAB BACKSTAGE WITH DAVID AT THE TACOMA DOME

Facing Page Below:
DRUMMER TONY THOMPSON WITH DAVID IN CHICAGO

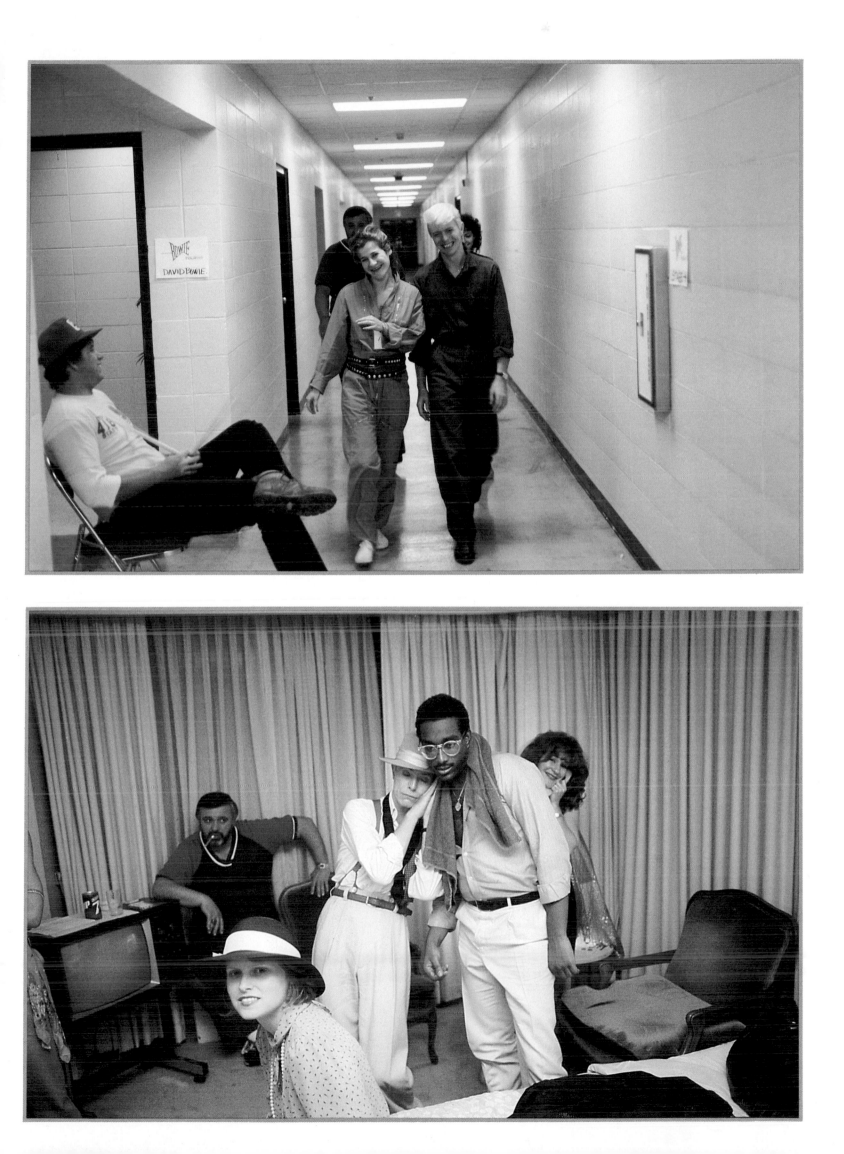

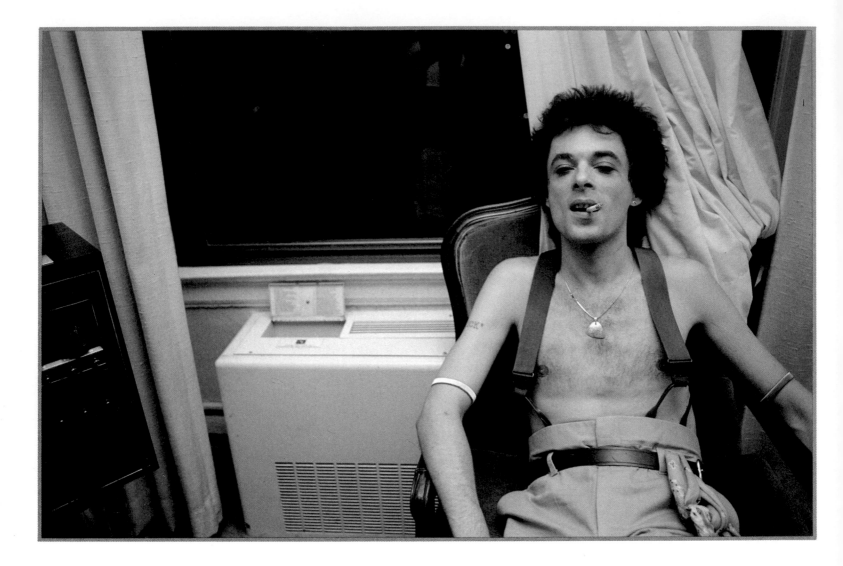

SLICK AFTER THE SHOW IN CHICAGO

EARL AND MARITA SLICK IN LOS ANGELES

DAVID'S ASSISTANT, COCO SCHWAB, BACKSTAGE IN CHICAGO

tips to waiters and all that. As me. Then he ran off with some film producer's wife and $500,000 of the film producer's money—as me—and flew to Hawaii. Where he promptly was greeted with banner newspaper headlines: 'BOWIE ARRIVES WITH PRODUCER'S WIFE.' Newspapers were doing a whole number on it. And I was in Scotland. This guy was flashing around a credit card in the name of David Bowie, and people were of course accepting it. So all this money was being spent in my name. The newspapers wouldn't believe it wasn't me. They insisted it *was* me. And they said, well, if it's really not you, you contact us from wherever you are, because we know this is you. So I had to go through this great farce of phoning all these columnists and gossip writers and say, listen, check the lines, this is a call from David Bowie, and I have an international operator to prove it. It was quite absurd."

Was this one ever caught?

"Oh, yes, they caught him. Now, this is the great thing. He got the idea to do it when he was in reform school. His cellmate was a Jimi Hendrix clone! Isn't that great? I thought that was wild. There's a clones movie in there somewhere. But he was the most extraordinary one. I still get letters saying, 'You probably remember when you had dinner at my house,' and on and on and worse. There were a few clones in London, very smartly turned out, who already had the little moons sewn onto their jackets. They must have been up sewing all night. Oh dear." A hearty laugh and then he's off to play Baker Street with Joey.

Eric announces "Showtime, lads." Joey gives his father a "police escort" down the corridor on a wheeled equipment case. Fan squeals start the minute Bowie's blond tresses move into sight. There is a heavy, visible, floating cloud of very strong marijuana smoke in the air, what is sometimes called "polio weed" in this part of the country. Bowie's biggest cheer comes when he takes a deep inhale onstage and says, "My, don't you smell good!" At halftime, in his dressing room, David laughs: "We've never smelled an audience like this before. I got a contact high from just breathing. I looked down there and saw all those eyes at half-mast and I said, oh boy, we've got a show ahead of us."

As he went out in his lime green suit for the second half, fans hanging over the railings yelled, "David! David, we love you! Invite us to your party!" "I don't have a party," he coyly replied. "Do you?"

The show goes very well. The most interesting item thrown onto the stage is a note with a phone number. The note says "Even a date can be a special event."

The Getaway from the Superdrum is fast, and JET is airborne from Austin, Dallas-bound at 11:26 p.m. Little talk on the plane—everyone is exhausted—and a quick dinner of barbecue ribs and chicken and pecan pie before regaining the sanctuary of quiet rooms at the Mandalay. As JET lands in Dallas, at precisely midnight, Amy shouts, "Pool party!"

JACLYN SMITH IN LA

HENRY WINKLER AND JIM KATZ IN LOS ANGELES

Do you remember President Nixon
Do you remember the bills you have to pay
or even yesterday

YOUNG AMERICANS

BOWIE, BACKSTAGE, ABOUT TO GO ON IN DETROIT

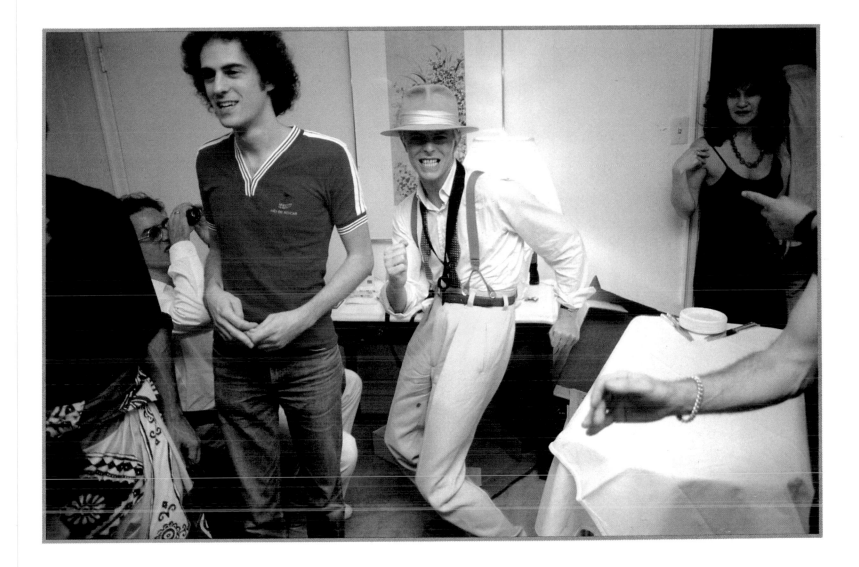

AFTER-SHOW PARTY AT CHICAGO'S AMBASSADOR EAST HOTEL

JET 24 IN PARIS

AN ITALIAN DINNER SERVED ON JET 24 ALOFT

CHINESE FAN IN TOKYO

BOWIE FANS AT BUDOKAN, TOKYO

I N A PERFECT ROCK & ROLL
world, the Moonlight '83 did its damnedest to be the first rock tour to
hit forever. Texas rolled into Norfolk, this smooth and well-oiled
machine-cum-caravan-of-gypsies pulling in 21,370 paying clients.
"CHARISMATIC BOWIE DELIVERS," the newspaper headline said. Then on to
Largo (29,471) and Hershey 25,230) and Foxboro (60,000) and on and
on and on through Toronto and here and there and everywhere.
Newspaper reviews pretty much fell into line like a row of dominoes:
the last crucial review city had been LA. And the very crucial Robert
Hilburn of the LA *Times* had weighed in with a hosanna: "For Bowie, a
triumph of heart and soul." Hilburn was God-blessed by many
members of the troupe for his holy endorsement. Mikal Gilmore's luke
warm elevation in the LA *Herald-Examiner* was levened somewhat by
his referring to the tour as "Mysterious Moonlight."

Off to Vancouver to tape a Home Box Office special and to
Winnipeg, where the Winnipeg *Sun* somewhat charmingly turned over
one whole edition to Bowie. He filled the front page with a photo and a
screaming banner headline: "TONIGHT IS THE NIGHT: BOWIE!" Anxious fans
were informed that Bowie now smokes Marlboros, did a duet of "Little
Drummer Boy" with Bing Crosby, and seems to have no current,
constant romantic companion. After the concert, the *Sun* trumpeted
"BOWIE: NOW WE'VE HEARD EVERYTHING!!!!!" The Bowie show filled up the first
five pages, with details of everything about "the rock event of the
decade." Nothing was too unimportant to document: whether it was
the fact that 50 bikers wearing T-shirts emblazoned with "Please Feel
Secure" were frisking concertgoers at the door or the local realtor Gary
Bachman (brother of Randy of Bachman-Turner Overdrive) loaned his
1981 champagne-colored Mercedes 350 to Bowie to the claim by the
Sun's staff that Bowie's sound could be heard in the *Sun* plant, on
Church Avenue, three miles away from the stadium. The North
American finale is, fittingly, a Bill Graham blowout (57,920 looking on)
at Oakland Stadium on September 17th, with parties galore.

Time off now—almost a month off—so much time off that it made
everyone a bit nervous and eager to regroup in Tokyo for the onslaught
of the Pacific Campaign. Tour members flew into Tokyo by October 16

Facing Page:
JAPAN'S YOKOHAMA STADIUM, OCTOBER 25,
1983

WHAT HAPPENS IN A TOKYO RESTAURANT

C

190

My little china girl
You shouldn't mess with me
I'll ruin everything you are
I'll give you television
I'll give you eyes of blue
I'll give you man who wants to rule the world

CHINA GIRL

for a production meeting before the two-week-blitz of Tokyo, Yokohama, Osaka, Nagoya, and Kyoto. Bowie's press conference at the Akasaka Prince Hotel may have set a world record for the number of strobe lights going off at once: it was like a fireworks show with 300 or so cameramen firing away. Bowie draped Japanese phrases over the interviewers, and they practically melted with delight. "Oishii desu," Bowie said, "sake o kudasai. I became interested many years ago in kabuki and noh. Then I started visiting here in the late Sixties as tourist and performer. I've always had a strong affinity for the East." Japan was his. The shows were sold out. Special police had to rush him and his entourage onto trains. But the beautiful part was that—more so than in the States or Britain—David could walk the streets almost as an ordinary citizen and stop in shops and eat out and pretty much go about his business without overly worrying about being a superstar.

Even so, audience response to the concerts is remarkable. Ordinarily orderly Japanese fans become out-of-order and try dancing in the aisles. Even the reviews are consistently praiseworthy. Dozens of young Japanese men show up at Bowie concerts sporting flamingly dyed yellow hair like Bowie's. It's called the "Bowie Cut," and it's suddenly No. 1 in Japanese hair salons. Although virtually every Japanese publication runs flattering—almost embarrassingly so—reviews of Bowie's show, there is a conservative backlash. The Weekly *Yomiuri* printed what it called "A Study of the Pathological Influence on Japanese Society by the Arrival of Rock World Superstar David Bowie." This is part of it: "It has become very fashionable for popular male entertainers in Japan to dye their hair blond and wear makeup.... The originator of this fad is the British rock singer David Bowie.... He has even attracted adult women (as opposed to just teeny boppers). At his press conference on the 18th, 'female journalists,' whom we never see at press conferences, crowded around and, although there was an interpreter present, these women asked questions in their pidgin English. It was disgusting."

Not disgusting enough, obviously, to ruin a spectacular rock & roll tour. Fans—12,000 fans—packed into the Budokan for the first Japanese concert on the evening of October 20. Tickets that had sold for 6,000 yen were being scalped for upwards of 30,000 yen. The 8,000 programs costing 1,800 yen each quickly disappeared. Nagisa Oshima, who had directed Bowie in *Merry Christmas, Mr. Lawrence*, was in the crowd, along with actress Keiko Matsuzaka and singers Miya Takagi and Naomi Akimoto. Reviews for the shows by this suddenly dubbed "Japanologist superstar" were predictably feverish: such words as "dazzling" were thrown about quite a bit. Matsuzaka, a superstar in Japan in her own right, even said that her own work on stage might be changed after seeing Bowie perform and feeling his "essence."

Band members who had not visited Japan before were surprised on a couple of counts. One said the reverence Bowie was accorded bordered on "sheer idolatry." They also were not used to relatively disciplined audiences, who, on the one hand waited patiently to be guided to their

DAVID WITH JAPANESE SINGER SANDI (OF THE SUNSETS)

DAVID SITTING IN ON TOKYO RADIO

seats by flag-bearing ushers and on the other hand left the hall knee-deep in paper streamers they hurled at the stage. And the train trips were manic. The band always boarded the train first and settled into a reserved car. Then police tried to sneak Bowie—in dark glasses and overcoat—furtively on board. Hysterical kids always seemed to figure out who the mystery man with the blond hair was. Odd.

Japan down, Australia up. Off to Perth and a warm welcome. Bowie has been an Australian favorite for years, long before he filmed his acclaimed video of "Let's Dance"—with its sympathetic portrayal of aborigines—here. At Perth Airport, Bowie stopped to sign autographs and then was off to what he said would be his "first and only" press conference during the Australian tour. If his experience with Tom Prior is any gauge, then it seems Bowie can grease any skids. Prior is a columnist for the *Sun* of Melbourne. He has four young daughters, and he does not like Bowie records. His lasting memory of Bowie had been of him "in drag, with high heels, white stockings and crotch-hugging tights." Believe Prior when he says: "I came to the press conference to jeer, not to worship. But if Bowie didn't win me, he came close. Like the captain of the premiership side, he is an honest man." After Bowie spoke—honestly—about sex, other sex, drugs, his son, nuclear war, and the fate of the aborigines and how he would like to revive the idea of the Brotherhood of Man, Prior (not quite an old fart) concluded that "Mary, my remaining unmarried daughter, can play and replay the remaining Bowie records in peace from now on."

A fitting summation of Bowie's conquest of the land down under, a still turbulent and free-spirited land where justice is often of the two-fisted kind and where a British rock star might not expect to find the welcome mat left out. But his public reception and his critical notices throughout Australia were largely of the caliber that flacks like to call "fabulous, at the very least." The *News* of Adelaide merely called Bowie's concert at the Adelaide Oval "the show of the decade." The main controversy was in Brisbane, where promoter Paul Dainty gambled $50,000 of his own money on the sound of Bowie's show. The sound level, that is, the sound in decibels. Before permitting the show, in Lang Park, the City Council had demanded that Dainty post a $50,000 bond as insurance against excessive volume from the show. Residents on Charlotte Street and Red Hill and Milton and Castlemaine even held Bowie parties to hear—or not hear—the noise from Bowie's show. They did not. Dainty's bond was saved. Brisbane's Lord Mayor Alderman Roy Harvey was not surprised, since he was at the show, meeting Bowie. "I liked him," said Alderman Harvey. "I found him to be a very down-to-earth guy."

Bowie's farewell to Australia came during The Getaway after a show before 25,000 in Sydney: while Bowie & Co. zoomed away from the Sydney showground the night of November 19—and while the crowd stamped and clapped for an encore—fireworks split across the night sky to spell out: Goodnight Sydney and Thank You Australia.

Preceding Pages:
PHOTO CALL AT THE TOKYO PRESS CONFERENCE

CHECKING OUT THE FOOD IN TOKYO

THIS IS HOW EARL SLICK LOOKS

PART OF THE AUDIENCE IN YOKOHAMA

On to New Zealand, home of Bowie tour wardrobe stylist Glenis Daly and also of many Bowiephobe fears. Glenis made the tour feel at home. Bowiephobes didn't. His show at Wellington's Athletic Park before 50,000 or so boisterous fans was described by one local critic as worthy of knighthood. But neighborhood residents complained of hooliganism and communicated their fears to Auckland, where Bowie's next show was scheduled. Meanwhile, the Toarangtira Tribe of the Maori culture, with a long heritage of proud independence, decided that Bowie was a like warrior and invited him and his band to a formal tribal ceremony. (First rock star in history to be so honored, for those of you keeping score.) The ceremony was semi-sacred: not many are invited within the walls. It was almost a blessing.

Wellington was not. It was a wild crowd, bottle-throwers included, and David even had to stop the show at one point when security told him a person was down and not being attended to.

On to Auckland. The advance press is spectacular: "RESIDENTS FEAR BOWIE RAMPAGE" reads one banner headline. "ENJOY IT BUT BEHAVE PLEA FROM BOWIE" is another. Apparently, Auckland residents are catching a contagion from Wellington residents, who are allergic to Bowiefans. They do, on the other hand, have some evidence of disgusting public acts allegedly perpetrated by alleged Bowiefans. Wellington residents were described as being in a "very deep mood of sullen anger" over public vomitus and urination. So what do you do?

Enjoy it, but behave, that's what. "We are going to have a good time," Bowie said, "just as long as people don't throw bottles and act like hooligans." Behave, he said.

And they did in Auckland, 90,000 or so, with their bonfires up on the hills around the site. Looking like Huns in the flickering firelight but behaving.

Great cheers when Bowie released two white doves, as a statement about the nuclear arms race. (Being prudent, the doves flew back and were returned to their home.) Tour officially over, Bowie threw a party, with Polynesian dancing girls. Since he had decided to go on and do a "Bungle in the Jungle" stripped-down-to-the-basics tour without most of the crew, he asked the road crew to cut the huge cake-shaped-like-the-earth.

Next day, fly to Singapore. David wanted to play Singapore, Bangkok, and Hong Kong. He will throw a financial loss with these concerts but, what the hey, he enjoys the new horizons. He is also totally unrecognized walking the streets in those three cities. The shows were also quite different. No more costumes and staging and vari-lites, for one thing; but in Singapore, the police decreed that there must be a vacant area about 60 feet across between the stage and the audience. There was a tiny ramp reaching out to the crowd that Bowie and Slick and Carlos took turns venturing out on. Very sedate in Singapore. On to Bangkok. The plane aborted its landing and nosed up and accelerated at the last minute. The pilot actually explained that there was another

Facing Page:
"CRACKED ACTOR" IN JAPAN

Following Pages:
PART OF THE CROWD IN NAGOYA, JAPAN

THE PROFFERED FLOWERS START TO GO NEAR THE END

IT WAS COLD IN OSAKA; HENCE, THE LEG WARMERS

A FLOWER FROM A FAN IN TOKYO

plane in the flight path. "Happened to me last time I was here," said Frankie Enfield to white-faced companions. At the airport, a flat-bed truck loaded on the luggage and everyone was off to the President Hotel.

President Hotel, which mostly succeeds in its valiant effort to offer Western luxury in the midst of Eastern deprivation. Your big rockshows don't come to Bangkok every day, and for good reason. No reason to expect a rock & roll tradition in what was once the imperial capital of Siam. David put on his show in the army's stadium, the only one big enough to hold a rock multitude, and he had to airlift in electrical and sound equipment from all over the Far East to patch together an adequate rock-stadium sound. And it was one hell of an event for Thailand's rock-starved fans. This, the largest rock concert in Thai history, was set for the king's birthday, and George Simms had prepared a special concert introduction that he delivered in credible Thai and David wished the king a happy birthday and the fireworks display after the show was but a crown on an evening of royal entertainment.

Bangkok was a grand diversion on the tour. David embarked on a day-long, gondola tour up the majestic Chao Phraya River, past the exotic floating markets and to fabled Buddhist temples.

Off to Hong Kong. A calm, cosmopolitan close to a record-breaking tour. After the first night's show on December 7 at Hong Kong Coliseum, the Hong Kong Urban Council complained to promoter Rigo Jesu that the business of Bowie kicking a world globe out into the crowd caused "unruliness" and ought to be stopped. The next night, David kicked *two* globes out. During "Modern Love," the song that concluded Serious Moonlight '83, there was ordered chaos. Frank Simms and Carmine had raided the lockers and started hurling towels by the handful into the crowd. Then, infectiously, everyone onstage started throwing anything they could grab: hats, picks, you name it. The tech crew came out onstage to dance, and about 50 members of the audience jumped onstage to do the same. Some of the kids were hauled up by David, for a fitting farewell to Tour '83.

Later, the hottest ticket in Hong Kong was the goodbye party at the Hollywood Boulevard disco. It was a sedate, introspective affair with champagne and Chinese food and a brief appearance by David. Welcome to the rock of the Eighties.

BOWIE AND FLOWERS FROM FANS, TOKYO

Facing Page:
"CRACKED ACTOR" IN JAPAN

GEORGE SIMMS FLANKS A VIEW OF THE BAND'S DRESSING ROOM

DAVID BACKSTAGE IN MELBOURNE

ADELAIDE, AUSTRALIA, WAS A LOOSE, FUN, SHOW

Facing Page:
RAIN DURING "JEAN GENIE" AT THE ADELAIDE OVAL

Following Pages:
BOWIE DOES A CLIP FOR MTV AT MILTON KEYNES BOWL

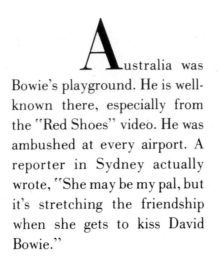

Australia was Bowie's playground. He is well-known there, especially from the "Red Shoes" video. He was ambushed at every airport. A reporter in Sydney actually wrote, "She may be my pal, but it's stretching the friendship when she gets to kiss David Bowie."

THIS IS THE STADIUM IN SYDNEY

A RECORD STORE IN SYDNEY

"THE FINEST WHITE PERFORMER ALIVE," WAS ONE U.K. REVIEW

Facing Page:
"CHINA GIRL" FOR THE CROWD AT MILTON KEYNES BOWL

Here am I floating round my tin can,
Far above the moon,
Planet Earth is blue
And there's nothing I can do.

SPACE ODDITY

THE MILTON KEYNES BOWL CROWD WELCOMES BOWIE'S GLOBE

Facing Page:
"SCAREY MONSTERS (AND SUPER CREEPS)"

MILTON KEYNES BOWL WAS THE MOST
TALKED-ABOUT SHOW

BACK-UP VOCALIST FRANK SIMMS

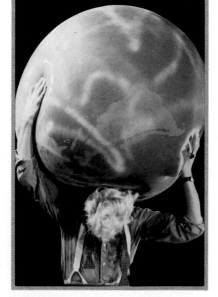

DAVID TAKES THE WORLD ON HIS SHOULDERS
AT WEMBLEY ARENA

Facing Page:
"CHINA GIRL" AS SEEN AT MILTON KEYNES
BOWL

Preceding Pages:
50,000 FANS AT MILTON KEYNES BOWL IN
ENGLAND

Following Pages:
THE MAMMOTH SHOW AT WESTERN
SPRINGS, AUCKLAND, N.Z.

The "Bungle in the Jungle Tour" became a very big deal. After all, which rock & roller last toured Singapore, Bangkok, and Hong Kong? Probably New Joy, a California band that opened for David in Singapore. David is quite the devotee of the Far East and spent much of his time just figuring out where to go, restaurant-wise.

DAVID VISITED SEVERAL TEMPLES IN SINGAPORE

ARRIVING IN SINGAPORE

EVERYBODY LIKED HANGING OUT AT RAFFLES IN SINGAPORE

Facing Page:
HIGH TEA AT RAFFLES HOTEL IN SINGAPORE

Following Pages:
THE CORRECT HAT TO WEAR AT SINGAPORE'S RAFFLES

Let's Dance
Put on your red shoes and dance the blues
Let's dance
To the song they're playin' on the radio

LET'S DANCE

As a hall of fame item, "Bungle in the Jungle" is a definite contender. Bowie was certainly the first rock & roller to go up-river from Bangkok. And to come back and play a show. It was on the King's birthday, and David wished him a happy one forever. George Simms did his concert introduction in Thai. A terrific fireworks show followed performance.

Facing Page:
TEMPLES IN SINGAPORE WERE A MUST-SEE

Following Pages:
TEMPLE-VISITING IN SINGAPORE

LOUNGING AT RAFFLES IN SINGAPORE

BREAKFAST IN THAILAND

THIS IS ARRIVAL IN BANGKOK

AT THE PRESIDENT HOTEL IN BANGKOK

Viewing a witch doctor's domicile in Bangkok

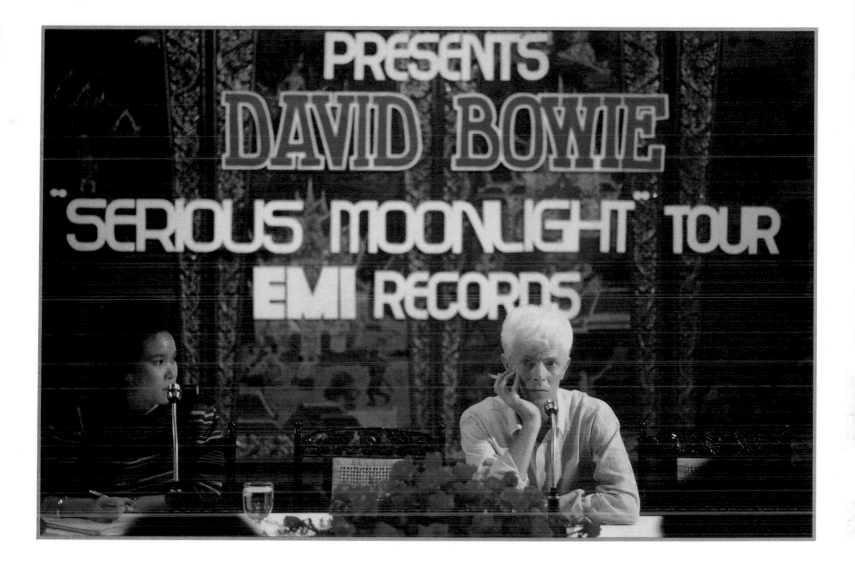

THE PRESS CONFERENCE IN BANGKOK

MONK OBSERVED NEAR A BANGKOK TEMPLE

DAVID'S WATERSIDE VISIT TO A BANGKOK TEMPLE

Luncheon taken near Bangkok

Facing Page:
ADRIFT ON THE CHAO PHRAYA RIVER IN THAILAND

DINING OUT IN TOKYO

BOATING IN HONG KONG'S HARBOR AT NIGHT

Following Pages:
A STAY AT HONG KONG'S HARBOUR VIEW HOLIDAY INN

"GOLDEN YEARS" DONE FOR THE LAST TIME IN HONG KONG

Facing Page:
"PLANET EARTH IS BLUE AND THERE'S NOTHING I CAN DO"

Following Pages:
THE TOUR'S END IN HONG KONG

LOVE LETTER FROM A 13-YEAR-OLD

Dear
    David Bowie,

I Love you very much.
I would Love if you sent
a picture of you to me.
I saw you at scope. I am
13 year old. My most favorite song
is Putting out the Fire with gasoline.
Me and my friend talk about you
all the time. I have a paster
of you in my room. I saw you
on the news. So would you sent
me a picture of you.

    I Love you.

                    Sabrina